Praise for *Greenthink*

"*Greenthink* is a gift to all of us and offers a solid platform for moving forward with positive, sustainable results. The idea that environmentalists and business should—and must—work together to assure optimum solutions is key to future success for all parties. A 'win-win,' Rick points out clearly, as we all share common enemies: waste, inefficiency, pollution, climate change, resource scarcity, and environmental degradation. To address these issues, embrace *Greenthink*."

—Art Gensler, Founder, Gensler

"One of the most significant arguments for sustainability I have ever come across. Rick's approach to this topic is different from any work to date, demonstrating the power of profitability and the simple case for why adopting 'green' principles is no longer just a choice, but a necessary edge to survive competitively in business."

—Paul Scialla, Founder and Chairman, DELOS Living

"With *Greenthink*, Rick Fedrizzi brings much needed clarity, coherence, and urgency to this generation's singular opportunity to align behind a common set of shared values that underscores the universality of human health and environmental quality, with transparency and reporting driving massive innovation as cornerstones of a prosperous future for all."

—Gail Vittori, Codirector, Center for Maximum Potential Building Systems

"*Greenthink* describes the philosophical underpinnings of the U.S. Green Building Council—but it goes much further to make the case that protecting the environment and prospering in business can go hand-in-hand. Along the way, Rick Fedrizzi recounts fascinating—sometimes funny—anecdotes about the history of the paradigm-changing organization he helped to create and shares stories from the business and environmental communities that amplify his important message."

—Alex Wilson, Founder, BuildingGreen, and President, Resilient Design Institute

"Kudos to Rick for brilliantly summing up an idea that we passionately embrace at SLOAN. *Greenthink* is how global leadership companies win, and it's how we'll deliver the safe, healthy, prosperous, and sustainable pl.... future deserves."

—Jim Allen, President and CEO, SL(

"*Greenthink* is a must-read if you care a future of Earth, our home. Rick Fedriz and personal story that *profit* is the sol ment-builder, and prophet."

—David Gottfried, CEO, Regenerative Ventures & Gottfried Institute, and Founder, U.S. and World Green Building Councils

"Rick has built the world's most impactful social enterprise in the U.S. Green Building Council and global green building movement. If you're looking for a roadmap for how to change the world by transforming markets, then look no further. This is it."

—Michelle Moore, CEO, Groundswell

"I love Rick's premise that we need both a sustainability mindset and sustainable streams of capital and ideas to get at the crux of our environmental issues, and that premise is proving out every day in green schools. Continuing to invest in the raising of a generation of sustainability natives is how we are achieving both social leaders and business leaders, and *Greenthink* lays out the best case I've seen yet for that!"

—Jayni Chase, Author of *Blueprint for a Green School*, and Advisor, Center for Green Schools at USGBC

"LEED challenged the status-quo thinking of architectural practice and laid the cornerstone for how our profession—and our buildings and communities—evolved these last two decades. *Greenthink* is quintessential Rick, and captures his optimism and boldness. Fearless and relentless in his passion, and with feet in both the business and environmental camps, his leadership has been key to keeping all the stakeholders in the conversation to collaborate our way to a much better future."

—Bob Berkebile, Principal, BNIM

"Environmentalism used to be a one-sided victory, but now it's a win-win. Businesses can do well by doing good and *Greenthink* is an important primer. Making money and protecting the planet not only aren't incompatible, they fit perfectly together. *Greenthink* explains how."

—Jeff Birnbaum, Journalist and Author of *Showdown at Gucci Gulch* and *The Money Men*

"Rick's passion for a better future and his work in forming and elevating USGBC has made sustainability a baseline requirement for top quality real estate. We share this passion and believe that a sustainable approach to real estate makes good business sense, helps the environment, and creates genuinely better places for people. Rick has proven his commitment to the green building community, and *Greenthink* is a testament to his dedication. Required reading for anyone in real estate."

—Gerald Hines, Founder and Chairman, Hines

GREEN
THINK

GREEN THINK

HOW PROFIT
CAN SAVE THE PLANET

RICK FEDRIZZI

CEO & FOUNDING CHAIRMAN
U.S. GREEN BUILDING COUNCIL

DISRUPTION
BOOKS

Published in the United States by Disruption Books.

ISBN 978-1-63331-005-6

Printed in the United States of America

Cover Design by Doyle Partners
Interior Design by Kim Lance

First edition

For Cathy, Nina, and Nate . . .

And for my father, Arigo Fedrizzi,
who taught me that most problems in life can
be solved by a long walk in the woods . . .

CONTENTS

AUTHOR'S NOTE

This book is not just *about* sustainability—it *is* sustainable. On average, the book industry emits 8.85 pounds of carbon to publish a single book and, by some estimates, about one billion of the four billion books printed each year are never sold or read. That's a lot of wasted paper, not to mention the countless tons of wasted water, chemicals, and oil used to manufacture and distribute all those unread books. But rest assured, this book was printed on demand. That's right—we printed this copy just for you, because there's no reason to print more books than will be read or to use more resources than we need. Printing on demand is less wasteful, that's for sure. But it's also less expensive for the publisher of this book and more profitable for the author. And because the proceeds from *Greenthink* will go straight to the U.S. Green Building Council's Project Haiti and Center for Green Schools initiatives, that's something you can be happy about, too. I've also tried to keep this book short and sweet, both to reduce the amount of resources used and to get on with the important work ahead.

—R. F.

FOREWORD

By LEONARDO DiCAPRIO

WE ARE LIVING DURING a period of change unprecedented in the history of our planet.

Let me repeat that: *unprecedented in the history of our planet.*

Humanity's impact on our environment and our climate will shape the future of life on Earth. *All* life. And not in some distant epoch, but during your lifetime and those of your children. The choice before us now—to act with urgency, or to continue our ecological downward spiral—will determine nothing less than the survival of our civilization and the fate of millions of species.

My wakeup call came after meeting with former Vice President Al Gore when we sat down for a talk about the state of our environment. His crash course on climate change terrified and motivated me, setting into motion a personal commitment to learn as much as possible from leading scientists and activists about how to protect our planet for future generations.

These efforts have taken me to some of the most remote and beautiful places on Earth, where the effects of climate change are plain to see up close, but they're also so drastic that you can observe them from space. They're happening *now*, in real time, in our most critical ecosystems. And they're being exacerbated by the urban and suburban ecosystems where we spend the vast majority of our time. Buildings—like the ones where we work, sleep, and go to school—account for 40 percent of the world's energy consumption and a third of all greenhouse gas emissions. As our population continues to rise all around the world, new buildings are going up each and every day.

In 2007, I worked alongside some of the world's most brilliant scientists, leaders, and activists on a documentary called *The 11th Hour,* about global warming and the rapid decline of our planet's life systems. That's how I met Rick Fedrizzi. Rick knows just how large a role our buildings and cities play in the climate change crisis. And he has succeeded where so many others have failed in galvanizing support and making progress on critical environment issues, most notably by cofounding and leading the U.S. Green Building Council (USGBC).

Due in large part to the vision and efforts of Rick and USGBC, green building represents nearly 40 percent of new construction globally, and by 2020 green construction is predicted to be valued at around $3.8 trillion. Add to this the significant efficiency upgrades underway in existing buildings, and that's billions of tons of carbon emissions avoided. Green building offers the single largest, most immediate impact we can make in the battle against climate change—not to mention the promising innovations that have been developed and the new green jobs created.

Today, green building is arguably the world's largest and most successful environmental movement, and it's no exaggeration to say that Rick's work has been revolutionary. The strategy he has championed—the call to action at the heart of this book—has the potential to change the world.

When I first met Rick, I was immediately impressed by the depth of his knowledge and inspired by the depth of his passion—not just for buildings or the environment, but for people and our communities. Rick's activism is, above all, about his love of humanity. At one point, when we were filming *The 11th Hour*, Rick spoke about a future where, as he put it, "buildings are used as sanctuaries for human health." Rick has done so much to advance us toward that future—to make that vision real and immediate and measurable. But he knows that green buildings are just one aspect of the vast change that's required to halt and reverse the devastating effects we continue to see all around us. And that's why this book is so important.

In these pages you will find a compelling history, a clear instruction manual, and most important, a convincing argument. By taking the principles that have made the green building movement so effective and extrapolating them to society at large, Rick offers a viable vision for saving the planet from humanity—and for saving humanity from itself.

That's why I urge you to read this book and then share it with everyone you know.

We need to demand more green buildings, and we need to apply more sustainable, green thinking to everything we do, because the clock is ticking. There's no time to waste.

A NEW NARRATIVE

"Face reality as it is,
not as it was or as you wish it to be."
—Jack Welch

NOT LONG AGO, I was sitting in my office, talking with a reporter from one of the big newspapers. I watched him open his bag and remove the tools of his trade, lining them up on the table the way a surgeon arranges her scalpels. Notebook, audio recorder, research documents, prewritten questions. It quickly became clear that he was intent on writing an exposé about the U.S. Green Building Council (USGBC), the organization I cofounded and now lead. He had prepared for a laborious extraction of our deep, dark secrets.

But it didn't take very long—I cut right to the chase.

"The way it works," I began, "is that developers, owners, and tenants see significant savings and environmental benefits from green buildings, while USGBC members see significant financial returns."

He glanced at the audio recorder he'd put on my desk, presumably to make sure its red light was still on. Then he looked back at me, his face showing a mix of bewilderment and disappointment—like a cat that has just been handed its mouse.

"It sounds like you're admitting," he said, "that USGBC members use environmental sustainability as a way to make money."

"That's *exactly* what they do!" I replied.

Needless to say, it was a short interview.

This reporter thought I was fessing up to a nefarious ploy—a greenwashing scheme of epic proportions. In fact, I was pointing out a fundamental truth about enterprise and the environment in the twenty-first century: *sustainability has become an incredible business opportunity.*

The guy may have been a journalist, but this was news to him. And he's not alone. I'm constantly confronted by—and confronting—people who just don't get who I am and what I do. You could say I stick out like a green thumb, thanks to my convention-bending belief that profit can (and hopefully will) save the planet.

Of course, by "save the planet," I don't mean the 4.5-billion-year-old space rock we call home. The rock will still be here even when people aren't. What I mean is that we must *save the world as we know it*—a world in which modern civilization is able to thrive. It has become abundantly clear at this point in human history that, if we want to continue to thrive, we must not exploit the natural world, but live and work in harmony with it.

Over the past twenty-plus years, I've worked hard to bring together a community of like-minded professionals who have the skills to turn the dream of a sustainable future into a profitable reality. USGBC's member organizations range from Fortune 500 companies to mom-and-pop design shops; our LEED professionals around the world include everyone from blue-collar contractors to white-collar start-ups. But no matter where they are or what they do, our members share a diehard belief that sustainability is a win-win for the economy and the environment.

Outside of the green building community, however, espousing this point of view is often met with a blank stare—if not fierce disagreement. After all, everyone knows the private sector and the environmental movement are mortal enemies, right? We read about businesses fighting environmental regulation because it threatens their profits, or environmental protesters putting themselves between greedy oil companies and their deep-water drilling rigs. It's an easy narrative to get your head around. Everyone has a clear, simple goal: making a buck by pillaging the Earth, or killing jobs to save some flora and fauna. It's an "either/or" scenario in most everyone's book. The idea that it could be "both/and" is, to the vast majority, unfathomable.

And that's no surprise. After all, this is how we've seen the world for the past fifty years. Environmentalists and business leaders know their friends and foes. It's clear who they need to "defeat" in order to "win." Sure, both sides have been cooperating a bit better as of late. Environmental groups monitor and verify the private sector's carbon emissions and other environmental impacts, for example. And almost every company aims to be *perceived* as green. But for the most part, environmental activists and the business community continue to wage the same battle they've been fighting for decades.

Here's the thing about this adversarial worldview: for a long time, it pretty accurately described the facts on the ground. The environmental movement was absolutely right that the only way to get business to lessen its impact on the environment was through the time-tested method of agitation, legislation, and regulation. Without the force of law, no amount of pleading could get the private sector to clean up its act. Industry had no incentive—and no desire—to give up profit and growth (as they were used to accounting for it) for a cause that wasn't their own. And the environmental movement knew it, so they protested and lobbied to pass major pieces of environmental legislation that we revere to this day: the Clean Air Act, signed by President Nixon in 1970; the DDT ban, which followed in 1972; the Clean Water Act, passed over President Nixon's veto that same year; the Montreal Protocol on CFCs in 1987; the Oil Pollution Act, signed by President George H.W. Bush in 1990, in response to the *Exxon Valdez* spill; and many more.

Meanwhile, the business community was right, too. What environmentalists were demanding was, essentially, a shifting of priorities away from profit and growth, and toward extreme environmental stewardship. And for businesses, these shifts seemed as unnecessary as they were expensive. The basic paradigm, as most everyone saw it, was that each unit of pollution kept out of the air, water, and land meant a unit of profit kept out of someone's pocket. And keep in mind, those pockets didn't belong just to CEOs. They belonged to everyone from money managers to office workers, from individual shareholders to pension funds, from universities to labor unions—anyone attached in any way to the vast web of the global economy.

In other words, the trade-offs weren't imaginary; they were real. The prevailing framework—economics vs. environmentalism— represented some very difficult choices. It's no surprise that policy makers have found it so hard to balance these competing priorities over the years.

Today, this much hasn't changed: environmentalism and industry are still pitted against each other, victims of a half-century of groupthink. On any given measure, one side automatically argues that doing X will kill the economy, while the other side argues that *not* doing X will kill the environment. We're all familiar with this murderous metaphor. In fact, a study from the Institute for Policy Integrity found that the use of the term "job-killing regulations" has dramatically increased in newsprint, from only four instances in 2007 to 706 in 2011—and as we enter the 2016 election cycle, it feels like 706 times a day. Sometimes it's more than just rhetoric.

U.S. Senator Joe Manchin famously said in a campaign ad that he would "take dead aim at the cap-and-trade bill"—and then he literally shot a bullet through it.

This narrative is all around us, every day and practically everywhere you look. Sometimes you hear different versions. On MSNBC, the environmental movement is the hero of the story. On Fox News, the CEO is the hero. And while the protagonists and antagonists differ, the plotlines are fundamentally the same. Both are passionate, partisan, polarizing defenses of deeply ingrained world views. Both reflexively assume that capitalism and environmentalism are forever at odds. Both cast the fight in terms of good and evil. But the most important commonality is this:

They are both wrong.

In the old narrative, what's bad for the environment is good for the economy, and vice versa. But take a look around! Environmental disasters are severely impacting the private sector. For instance, 2012 saw the most extensive U.S. drought recorded since the 1930s, resulting in $17.3 billion in lost crops. And on a single night that same year, Hurricane Sandy caused an estimated $65 billion in damage, including about $20 billion in lost business during the days that followed. Sure, Sandy was a "superstorm," a supposedly once-in-a-lifetime event. But who could fail to notice that severe weather is becoming more frequent and more costly with each passing year? According to the National Oceanic and Atmospheric Administration, in 2014 alone, eight weather and climate disasters in the United States cost more than $1 billion *apiece*. And whether you are living on the coast, working in insurance, or just thinking like a concerned citizen, that number is pretty terrifying.

Even if you write off the increasing impact of severe weather as some sort of meteorological fluke, the impact of pollution is impossible to deny. In fact, the World Health Organization (WHO) estimates that air pollution contributed to around seven million premature deaths globally in 2012, stating, "Air pollution is now the world's largest single environmental health risk." What the WHO doesn't say is that air pollution is also an *economic* health risk. Consider how entire economies are silently suffering the effects of environmental drag. For example, China has seen incredible economic growth over the past several years—but what if I told you that growth could be even higher? The World Bank estimates that the cost of environmental degradation and resource depletion in China was nearly *10 percent of its GDP* in 2008. If China is any indication—and you can bet that it is—just imagine the economic impact of pollution across the entire planet.

It's painfully clear to me that we're in the midst of a global environmental depression. Tragically, few people understand this, because they believe the private sector and the environmental community are independent actors in a zero-sum game. This antiquated, adversarial worldview isn't just dumb; it's *devastating*—to the economy *and* the environment.

Think about it this way: Because the environmental movement still considers business its sworn enemy instead of its natural partner, it has utterly failed at the decisive moment of the most important environmental battle in history. There's a better chance that you'll get struck by lightning while reading this book than that Congress will pass a carbon tax in my lifetime. Global climate conventions and negotiations have unraveled on so many occasions, I've lost count. Why? Because generally speaking, environmentalists continue to antagonize industry instead of partner with it. As a result, business interests dig in their heels and stand in the way of agreements that could prevent catastrophic climate change.

Meanwhile, the private sector is leaving *trillions* on the table—not to mention condemning humanity and our planet to a terrifying future—by failing to widely embrace the extraordinary power of sustainability to drive economic growth. There are two key ways all businesses stand to gain from being environmentally conscious. First, by eliminating waste and doing things more efficiently, companies save money. Second, by using sustainability to drive innovation, new products become more effective, more desirable to customers, and thus more profitable.

Let me repeat that: More savings. More innovation. More customers. More money.

What's not to like here?

Unfortunately, the tired, old narrative through which most people understand the world, and the groupthink within business and environmental circles that sustains it, are preventing a lot of money from being made and a lot of planet from being saved. But a new narrative is emerging—a new way of thinking, even—that is rooted in reality, not distorted by history. While the old narrative claims that the environment is the enemy of growth, the new narrative holds that the environment and the economy are deeply, fundamentally connected. They share common enemies: waste, inefficiency, pollution, climate change, resource scarcity, and environmental degradation. They also share a common ally: sustainability. And instead of intractable, insulated groupthink, they share a common outlook: *greenthink.*

Greenthink occurs when businesses, nonprofits, governments, and individuals marry environmental and economic principles for the benefits they can receive from both. Throughout the global economy, a select number of enlightened companies are already engaged in greenthink by leveraging the power of sustainability to drive profits. These businesses aren't using less energy and fewer resources in the name of self-denial or out of the goodness of their hearts; they're *consuming less* in order to *earn more.* The economic incentives are changing, and so are the business models. The result is a measurable reduction in the damage that many companies inflict on the environment and people, an increase in the quality and desirability of their products and services, and a reward in the form that business understands best: cold, hard cash. In fact, preeminent management consulting firm McKinsey & Company says that "the choice for companies today is not if, but *how* they should manage their sustainability activities."

Conventional wisdom tells us that sustainability is prohibitively expensive; that industry is, by definition, destructive; and that environmentalism and capitalism are diametrically opposed. But it's time to toss that old way of thinking out a triple-glazed, energy-efficient window. Because even though the private sector and the environmental movement have long thought of themselves as adversaries, the truth is, they will share the same fate.

The future of the planet is at stake, and so is the future of the global economy. Environmental degradation and climate change are beginning to take an enormous economic toll that will grow by orders of magnitude in the coming years. Meanwhile, environmentally friendly business practices are creating an economic windfall for those smart enough to embrace them. This is the new reality—and our historic opportunity. Profit-driven strategies can bring us together and help us dramatically reduce our carbon footprint, eliminate harmful pollution, and build a better, greener world.

In other words, *profit can save the planet.*

Perhaps that sounds too good to be true. After all, if sustainability is so profitable that it *can* save the planet, why *hasn't* it? Why do we still see rampant pollution and cynical greenwashing from the vast majority of the private sector? The answer is simple: most companies aren't yet taking stock of the environment's impact on their bottom line. But I know this will change, because I've watched it happen to one of the world's largest, dirtiest industries: real estate.

In just over a decade, through the revolutionary, voluntary LEED certification program, USGBC and the private sector have channeled ingenuity, shared innovations, and transformed real estate and the building trades—two of the economy's largest sectors. To date, LEED has certified four *billion* square feet of sustainable real estate worldwide. Another ten billion square feet are in the development pipeline. That's a lot of square feet, but how does this translate into dollars and cents? USGBC commissioned Booz Allen Hamilton (BAH) to find out. According to BAH's 2015 *Green Building Economic Impact Study*, the green building sector (which includes LEED, ENERGY STAR, and other green-certified construction) contributed $167.4 billion to U.S. GDP from 2011 to 2014. By 2018, BAH projects that figure will nearly double, to $303.5 billion.

The green building movement has certainly made a lot of people a lot of money—something my reporter friend was fixated on, and rightly so. But let's be clear: we're not just talking about developers, manufacturers, and contractors. BAH found that, in 2015, the green building sector accounted for 2.3 million jobs, putting more than $134.3 billion in the pockets of American workers.

Of course, the environmental benefits of green building are just as significant as the economic ones. According to Paul Hawken, a legendary environmentalist, "USGBC may have had a greater impact than any other single organization in the world on materials saved, toxins eliminated, greenhouse gases avoided, and human health enhanced."

Not bad for a little environmental nonprofit organization.

The success of the green building movement has taught me two things. First, there is only one force powerful enough, and capable of working quickly enough, to reverse the trends eroding the environmental security of our planet and the future of humanity: *capitalism.* Second, greenthink is, simply put, the biggest and most incredible business opportunity of the twenty-first century.

That's why there are two messages at the heart of this book. If you're an environmentalist, it's time to face up to the limitations of the environmental movement, its strategies, and its methods—and it's time to start leveraging private-sector forces to drive change instead. And if you're a business leader, it's time to sustainably transform your enterprise before environmental factors—or your more sustainable competitors—put you out of business.

I'm writing this book for warmhearted conservationists *and* coldblooded capitalists, because profit *can* save the planet, and saving the planet will be *great* for business.

Let me show you how.

1

STICKERS FOR SUSTAINABILITY

"It's more fun to be a pirate than to join the Navy."
—*Steve Jobs*

IN THE EARLY 1990s, I was a young marketing executive at Carrier, one of the world's largest manufacturers of heating, air conditioning, and refrigeration systems. I had just moved back to New York after five years of selling air conditioners in Miami (which is harder than it sounds). There's no better training in the world to prepare a novice businessperson for a career in marketing than sales. Then again, all the sales experience in the world couldn't have prepared me for my first big marketing assignment.

I had recently been named Carrier's director of environmental marketing. Shortly thereafter, a new CEO came over from A Big Lighting Company. He had an idea, and his idea needed a marketer. So he went to my boss, the head of residential marketing, and asked for someone he could put on the job. Before I knew it, I was on my way upstairs to hear the new bigwig's big idea.

"Rick," the CEO said, "at my old company, I created an eco-lightbulb. I want Carrier to do the same thing for air conditioners."

Those words changed my life. But at the time, I had no idea what they meant. I didn't know what an eco-lightbulb was—nor did very many people back then. So I went to the hardware store and bought one. The first thing I noticed was the packaging: brown, recycled cardboard, and graphics that had been printed using soy-based ink. So far, so good. Then I opened up the box and took out the bulb. To my untrained eye, it looked like a regular incandescent lightbulb. There was nothing "eco" about it that I could detect except for the box it came in. Looking back, I recognize this as a classic case of "greenwashing"—a term for when a company claims, for marketing purposes, that its product is more environmentally friendly than it really is. Of course, I didn't know enough about sustainability at the time to call it that. Instead, I called it as I saw it: a gimmick to sell more lightbulbs. And the impetus for the gimmick was easy to understand. Sell more lightbulbs—or air conditioners—and you make more money. Needless to say, making more money was good for Carrier, good for my boss, and good for me.

But any marketer worth his salt knows what I learned down in Miami—that before you can make a ton of sales, you have to do a ton of research. You need to know your target customers; you have to understand what they want, what they need, and how to deliver it in a way that's profitable for you and affordable for them. I was far from an expert in environmentalism, that's for sure. But I personally identified with the movement, and I knew that if my eco–air conditioner was going to be successful with consumers, it needed more than just a new box.

The next day, I went to the bookstore, looking for clues on how to make air-conditioning more environmentally friendly. Unfortunately, the environmentalism section I was hoping to scour wasn't really a section at all. It was more like two books: Rachel Carson's 1962 *Silent Spring* and Aldo Leopold's 1949 *Sand County Almanac*. Both are masterpieces. But try using them to build a better air conditioner.

I spent the next few weeks doing just that—attempting in vain to apply Carson's and Leopold's lessons to the world of condenser coils and blowers. And I kept running into the same problem: How do you create a profitable, sustainable air conditioner based on principles that regard profit and sustainability as incompatible? According to the prevailing philosophy of zero-sum environmentalism, the best thing Carrier could do for the environment was to sell an air conditioner that spit out lukewarm air—or better yet, to stop selling air conditioners altogether.

I wasn't about to take either of those ideas back to my CEO.

A short while later, out of desperation, and on a Friday night no less, I wandered into another bookstore. I wasn't really expecting to find anything. But there, staring me in the face, was a brand-new book just released that very week: *The Ecology of Commerce,* by Paul Hawken.

I picked it up and flipped through the pages. It was as though Hawken had written the book specifically for me. In fact, I would come to find out, Hawken *had* written the book for me, and for thousands of people like me—corporate executives who wanted to know how they could integrate environmental principles into their business practices. I devoured the book and, in doing so, found the answer to my big question. Hawken gave me a way out of the zero-sum trap. Not only were capitalism and environmentalism compatible, according to Hawken, they *depended* on each other.

It's a controversial idea today, but it was truly radical in 1993.

From a business standpoint, Hawken convinced me that the cynical, meaningless marketing of non-green products as environmentally friendly wasn't just profoundly deceptive—it was also profoundly *ineffective.* No one was going to pay more for any "green" product—a lightbulb, an air conditioner, or a solar panel—if it didn't do at least as good a job as what they already had. Even people with environmental preferences were basing their decisions primarily on performance.

I realized there was a much better way to sell more widgets and to earn more profits: by making a product that's better, period. Better for the environment, better for customers, better for the bottom line. Hawken argued that real profits and real efficiencies were interrelated. In order for both environmentalism and capitalism to be successful, they had to *combine* successfully. Neither needed to give up the fundamental attributes that made each one worthy on its own.

The idea was starting to gel. As far as my eco–air conditioner was concerned, the environmental benefits would have to be just as compelling as the marketing strategy. But I wanted, and needed, to learn more. *The Ecology of Commerce* showed me that there were some very smart people out there—Hawken foremost among them—who were working at the intersection of business and environmentalism. My next step was to find them.

First, I tracked down Amory Lovins, an energy efficiency guru, physicist, concert pianist, and all-around brilliant guy who founded an outfit called the Rocky Mountain Institute (RMI). Through Amory I met Bill Browning, another sustainability genius, who at the time worked for Amory at RMI. Then David Gottfried, who, with Browning, was exploring environmental issues with the American Society of Testing Materials (ASTM), tracked me down. David was a self-proclaimed disgruntled developer, an ideas guy who wanted to shake up the world. He was bored with real estate and frustrated with the progress he was—or wasn't—making at ASTM.

Here were a bunch of scientists, businessmen, thinkers, and idealists, all trying to crack the same code I was working to decipher. So, I thought, why not get all this brainpower together in the same room and see what happens?

In April, we gathered in Squaw Valley, California, where I was putting on a conference for Carrier with members of the manufacturing trade press. The four of us—Amory, Bill, David, and I—took some time to talk about what we could do together. By the end of our meeting, I was convinced: the eco–air conditioner was the start of something much bigger.

More to the point, I knew what I had to do.

I flew back to Syracuse and went straight to my CEO's office. "We can do this," I said, "but we're going to do it right. We're not just going to throw some recycled-content packaging around the same old air conditioner and call it 'eco.' We're going to give our customers something they'll really want to buy."

"I don't care what you do," he replied. "Just do it by January."

That was the date of the ASHRAE trade show—a huge, international expo put on each year by the American Society of Heating, Refrigerating, and Air-Conditioning Engineers. Now I had a deadline, and a critical one at that. My boss made himself very clear: whatever I cooked up was going to be a major focus for the company. And what I was cooking up was, essentially, to turn one of Carrier's flagship products green in six months—just in time to unveil it to an international audience.

I had my work cut out for me—but I also had a plan to get it done. First, I needed to get our people to design more environmentally friendly air conditioners. Then, I had to market the heck out of them.

One by one, I started meeting with Carrier's engineers to discuss what they could do to make our air conditioners more sustainable. Most of them didn't have to think too hard to come up with an answer: "Get the hell out of my office." But a few of them sat and talked with me, excited by the idea of a new challenge.

As the engineers worked, I turned to my own area of expertise. I decided to create a rating system to showcase the new features of our new products. I asked one of the best graphic designers I knew to come up with logos for the different ways in which we were making our air conditioners more environmentally responsible. I wanted these logos to be cool, iconic, and instantly recognizable. There were six of them in all: indoor air quality, sound reduction, air distribution, refrigerants, energy efficiency, and material reduction/recycled content.

Everything was ready just in time for the trade show, which was held that year at the massive McCormick Place convention center in Chicago. The morning of the expo, I got to the trade show floor early, around 6 a.m., carrying a box of stickers. I proceeded to walk the floor, from one Carrier product to the next. If one of our air conditioners had improved its refrigerants, I slapped on a refrigerants sticker. If another had a new, more efficient compressor and had reduced its decibel level, on went the stickers for energy efficiency and sound reduction. Some air conditioners ended up with a bunch of stickers, some with only one, and some got none at all.

I should point out that this was not some fancy, consensus-based, peer-reviewed, rigorously tested rating system. I was just awarding stickers based on my best guess of the direction the products were (and should have been) heading. That was the whole plan—put stickers on air conditioners. Simple enough. But what happened next was incredible.

Later that morning, before the convention center doors opened, the Carrier product managers arrived to put the finishing touches on their booths. Within a minute, they were swarming me: "Why does that guy's product have four stickers but mine only has one?" "Why did I get two but not three?" "What do you mean I can't have a sticker because my product isn't energy efficient?" The same folks who'd been slamming doors in my face just a few months earlier were now complaining that they wanted more stickers!

Then the expo started, and in came the trade press. They flocked to the Carrier booth and more or less ignored all the other manufacturers' displays. They were obsessed with our stickers and wouldn't stop asking about them.

That's when I realized what the product managers had figured out instantly. My stickers conveyed more than sustainability metrics. They delivered more than product information about the devices they were stuck on. They represented something else, something bigger. These stickers weren't the industrial equivalent of handing out gold stars to competitive fourth graders. They were marks of prestige and quality that would drive sales. They were incentives. Finally it dawned on me: without realizing it, and in the most rudimentary fashion you could possibly imagine, *I had begun to create a brand.*

Just like that, Carrier began to change from the inside. The press wanted to know what was up with these new eco–air conditioners. Product managers wanted to out-green each other, to earn that recognition and the branding associated with it. My fellow marketers were eager to promote these new products that were getting so much attention and doing so well with our customers. And the competition . . . well, they were speechless!

All because of a few stickers.

But this was more than just a marketing gimmick, and totally different from the recycled packaging of my boss's eco-lightbulb. My stickers *meant* something; cursory as the rating system was, the stickers were backed up by the guts of the gadgets themselves. And most important of all, customers could tell. The stickers spoke a "language." Folks could look at the logo advertising a more efficient compressor and make the connection to the energy bill savings they would enjoy because of the improved technology they were purchasing. The air conditioners really *were* more sustainable. And with the new branding I had developed, they were also more desirable and therefore more profitable. This was the furthest thing from greenwashing. Carrier's new air conditioners were green on the outside and green on the inside—and the company was generating a lot of green as a result.

I had succeeded in making my CEO happy. After all, he

was just after sales. But suddenly, that goal was no longer paramount to me. Something bigger, much bigger, had opened up—a new goal and a new opportunity, based on an incredible discovery: Paul Hawken was right. Sustainability and profitability really do go hand in hand.

2

PERMISSION TO LEED

"Coming together is a beginning;
keeping together is progress;
working together is success."
—Henry Ford

WHILE I WAS WORKING ON AIR CONDITIONERS, David Gottfried and Mike Italiano were working on a project of their own: inventing a new, sustainable way to build real estate. It was a mind-bending idea, and it electrified me just thinking about it. After all, air conditioners were just one piece in the vast puzzle of our built environment. David and Mike wanted to sustainably transform each and every piece of that environment and link them together to build a new, green world.

David knew buildings well—really well—and Mike was an environmental lawyer who understood the regulatory landscape better than almost anyone. But, they needed someone who could help them develop their concept in a way that would attract the business community. That's where I came in.

In 1993, David, Mike, and I combined forces and started the U. S. Green Building Council. Our mission was to foster what I had seen up close and personal at the ASHRAE trade show—the incredible market opportunity for green building products. We weren't talking just air conditioners, but everything under the sun, from drywall to paint to energy-efficient lighting and water-efficient plumbing. The built environment, we realized, was a huge part of our economy, and it had an equally huge impact on the natural environment and human health. We decided to create an organization that raised awareness about and encouraged the growth of what was then the practically nonexistent green building industry.

It was a start-up environment—fast, messy, improvisational. We intentionally modeled our vision for USGBC not on well-established environmental organizations like the Sierra Club, the Audubon Society, and the Natural Resources Defense Council (NRDC), but after private-sector trade associations and professional organizations like ASHRAE and ASTM. Our idea was simple: bring companies large and small to the table with environmental activists and idealists. We wanted to create a dialogue, to see what conversations and innovations that kind of partnership could spark.

But instead of a spark, we were thrown right into the fire.

Early in his first term in office, President Bill Clinton announced an initiative called the "Greening of the White

House." The plan was to make the White House more energy efficient and sustainable—in the very earliest days of people really understanding what that meant, to the president's great credit. Bill Browning was managing the effort for Mark Ginsberg at the Department of Energy and the American Institute of Architects, and Bill brought in a first-rate group of environmental activists to work with him.

He also invited me. By this point, I was the director of environmental marketing at Carrier and the cofounder of USGBC. But to a crowd of environmental activists, I was still an outsider. I was a businessman. I was corporate. I represented the enemy—the big, bad profit-seekers who were wrecking the planet. I'll never forget our first meeting. The assembled environmental activists and leaders treated me like an interloper, an enemy spy, a dirty industrialist. To this group of enviros, I reeked of corporate interests and "team business." *An executive from a manufacturing company? And he's supposed to make things better around here?* That was the general reaction—until something a little strange happened.

It was a kind, if seemingly odd, gesture. Amory Lovins was in the room, and in the middle of our meeting he walked over to me, pretty much out of nowhere, and started to give me a shoulder rub. Maybe he could see that I was tense or that others in the room were, too. Fortunately, he ended up working out more than just a few knots. Amory knew me and my work. We had met several times since my first foray into sustainability at Carrier, and we had grown to really like and respect each other. Because of his incredible work on energy efficiency at RMI, Amory had major credibility in any environmentally inclined room. And so, just like that, with a quick shoulder rub, one of the alpha-environmentalists signaled to the other members of his pack that I was all right.

And here I'd been worried about rubbing people the *wrong* way.

It was far from the last time that USGBC would feel tension or suspicion in its relationships with other environmental groups. But it was then, the very first time, that I learned something fundamental about that tension: It was tribal—even primal. It came down to a very deep mistrust between people who spent their lives working on the environmental team and people who spent their lives working on the business team. People were wary of me for trying to do something unorthodox: play for both teams.

But that was the whole point. In order to build an industry from nothing—not an easy thing—David, Mike, and I spent years trying to get both sides in the same room, working together. We held meetings. We made phone calls. We wined and dined and pitched our idea. Like a lot of start-ups, USGBC endured several years of slow, uncertain growth. In time, we began to recruit our founding members. Carrier, a subsidiary of the sprawling United Technologies Corporation (UTC), was an obvious choice, and forward-thinking companies like Armstrong, Herman Miller, and Andersen Windows soon joined, too. A handful of the premier environmental organizations, including the Sierra Club, the NRDC, and Audubon, also came aboard early. I got Carrier to pony up $5,000 and, along with David's bar mitzvah savings account (no joke!), we were off to the races.

Not that we went anywhere fast. We started small, with only thirteen members at first. This group became our board of directors, and I took on the role of founding chairman. The board managed every little thing, from designing our brochures and logo to making fund-raising calls when we could find the time between our day jobs and other responsibilities. We were having fun and felt we were doing good work, but I won't lie—it was a slog.

It won't surprise you that one of our big struggles as an organization was to bridge the gap between the constantly warring factions of business and environmentalism. Both sides reflexively mistrusted us. The more one would warm up, the more suspicious the other would grow. This was a problem because we were a mission-based trade association *and* an environmental nonprofit at the same time. Our whole organization was premised on the idea that real progress and profits could be attained through industry and environmental activists working together. Perpetual animosity—and, perhaps more important, the decades of experience and groupthink that had convinced the two sides they had an incentive *not* to work together—was preventing our core innovation from gaining traction.

Fairly often in the early days, USGBC was accused, sometimes quite angrily, of selling out. Even the people we had brought to the table—people interested in our idea—had trouble working together. I remember one incident especially well. One of our board members was also the head of a prominent environmental group. In the middle of a meeting, he accused someone else at USGBC, who also led an environmental group, of being in bed with big business. That other USGBC member pounded the table and shouted something unprintable. The board member got up and walked out of the room. We never heard from him again.

With stories like that, it's probably not surprising that building our membership was hard. But, despite our struggles, we had an advantage: competition. Because we were trying to recruit businesses and we already had one giant—United Technologies—in our corner, we could go to another competitor and say, "You're not going to let UTC have this green building space all to itself, are you?" The prospect of being left out of a new and potentially profitable market sector usually got their attention.

Over the first several years, by leveraging that competitive spirit and doing a lot of hard work, we corralled a few dozen members. These early adopters realized the market opportunity, and the environmental opportunity, of green building. But the green building industry itself was still nascent. It was relatively unknown, even among real estate developers (who thought we were truly crazy) and folks in the building trades (who were equally perplexed). No one had considered that the umpteen components needed to build a building were a *product category* that could be radically improved. To put it bluntly, we were a trade association for an industry that didn't really exist. We needed to change that—but how?

In 1997, we found our answer. That year, we started to develop what would become the most transformative market-based tool in the history of the environmental movement: Leadership in Energy and Environmental Design, or LEED.

LEED is a rating system—kind of like a nutrition label on a box of animal crackers (my favorite prop when I started explaining it to the public). But instead of measuring calories and sugar content, LEED rates a building in six categories: energy, water, waste, indoor environmental quality, materials, and innovation. And unlike nutrition labels, LEED has *nothing* to do with the government. It's a 100 percent private-sector, market-driven program that's administered by USGBC through a consensus-based process and governed solely by industry participants.

LEED is technical in practice but really simple in concept. It's based on credits. The more credits you earn, the greener your building is. A project earns credits by achieving a certain sustainability goal, such as reducing energy consumption, using water more efficiently, incorporating sustainable materials, or reducing the amount of construction waste that ends up in a landfill. Developers can choose from a long list of credits in order to arrive at a combination that works best for their project. If you earn a certain number of credits, you achieve the basic "certified" level. A few more credits, and you receive

LEED Silver certification. If you meet even more criteria, you earn LEED Gold status. Even more, and you can proudly tout your building's LEED Platinum rating—the highest there is (for now!).

That's it. It's that simple. In fact, it's an awful lot like the stickers that I slapped on air conditioners at Carrier. LEED establishes sustainability goals, and if you meet them, instead of a sticker, you get a plaque to display on your building and the bragging rights associated with being green. Of course, you also get the economic and environmental benefits of actually *being* green, too. The difference, though, is that while the stickers I developed for Carrier were handed out based solely on my gut reactions, LEED is based on years of scientific study, empirical testing, and the input of hundreds upon hundreds of technical experts from around the world.

Our first iteration of LEED was based on some of the ratings systems that David had worked on with ASTM, and on work that Rob Watson, who managed the effort, had done as a longtime leader at the NRDC. Rob understood how consensus standards worked, and he led the charge with an amazing group of volunteer technical specialists. I brought to the table my leadership and marketing expertise from Carrier and, with the help of countless volunteers and experts from across the country, together we created something unprecedented: a brand for green buildings that unified the industry, and a private-sector rating system that transformed the market on a scale none of us could have imagined in our wildest dreams.

In 1997, USGBC had fewer than fifty members and only a five-figure budget, and green buildings were more of an idea than a reality. We were such a shoestring organization that at one point that year, David wrote a check to USGBC for $40,000 just to pay our staff (of one) and keep our tiny San Francisco office open.

Fast-forward to 2015. LEED has certified green real estate in 150 countries, and there are green building councils in more than 100 countries. In the U.S., LEED-certified buildings will realize $1.2 billion in energy savings over the next four years, and LEED-certified construction will contribute 1.1 million jobs to the U.S. economy.

Of course, if I left you with the idea that USGBC's contributions begin and end with LEED, I would be doing everyone a big disservice. Not only has LEED been growing tremendously fast, but so have a number of other tools—a whole movement—inspired by it.

One of the reasons people have embraced LEED is because it is third-party validated—and we wanted to make sure it stayed that way. In 2008, the Green Building Certification Institute (GBCI) was founded, with the support of USGBC, to provide independent oversight of professional credentialing and project certification for LEED. Seven years later, GBCI is LEED-certifying some 1.85 million square feet every single day and has accredited the skills of some 200,000 LEED professionals.

Given the power of certification—and the countless people

who've asked us for (I'm not making this up) LEED for cruise ships, LEED for food safety, even LEED for tree houses!—GBCI has been able to help us dramatically expand our scope and scale our outreach to other audiences. GBCI changed its name in 2014 to Green Business Certification Inc., and it's rapidly moving beyond LEED and the building footprint. GBCI now certifies sustainable sites—from residential landscaping to public parks—through a rating system called, appropriately, SITES (a.k.a. the Sustainable Sites Initiative). GBCI also certifies green and resilient microgrids using the Performance Excellence in Electricity Renewal (PEER) program, designed to empower building owners and power providers to use data to configure and operate their systems in conjunction with each other to maximize effectiveness. Not only that, but GBCI also offers certification services to a World Bank program called EDGE (Excellence in Design for Greater Efficiencies) that helps jump-start emerging economies on the path toward sustainability.

Certifying individual buildings and sites is critical, but that's just the beginning of the story. In 2009, economist Nils Kok and a small team of colleagues launched the Global Real Estate Sustainability Benchmark (GRESB), which compiles data to help institutional investors promote sustainable buildings not just one at a time, but across entire global real estate portfolios. Let me give you an idea of how big these portfolios are: GRESB's 2015 Survey included 707 participants, with $2.3 trillion in gross asset value and

61,000 assets covered. It's no wonder that GRESB was acquired by GBCI in 2014. By combining GRESB with the building-specific information found in USGBC's Green Building Information Gateway (GBIG), we have developed, for the first time, a full asset-to-portfolio sustainability measurement solution for the world's largest asset class. Not only that, but given the size of these portfolios, we now have the tools to make an even larger impact on the sustainability of our built environment.

That said, building performance is not limited to energy use or materials or even the physical building. More and more, we're focusing on the people *inside* the buildings—to make sure buildings are working not just for the environment, but also for their inhabitants.

In 2012, I met Paul Scialla at the Clinton Global Initiative. Like me, he was the cofounder of a real estate-focused organization, DELOS. And like USGBC and LEED, DELOS has pioneered a new standard for buildings: the WELL Building Standard. WELL is the first protocol of its kind to focus specifically on human wellness within the built environment. It prescribes a series of technology enhancements and performance-based measures across seven categories: air, water, nourishment, light, fitness, comfort, and mind. You might have noticed that some of these categories are the same ones we focus on in LEED; in fact, WELL builds on the health metrics in LEED and takes them to the next level.

You can appreciate that when I met Paul, the proverbial

LED lightbulb in my head was pulsing. If LEED paved the way for a sustainable transformation in our built environment, I thought, WELL could spark a human health transformation on a similar scale. So I approached Paul and his twin brother, Pete, and I was beyond impressed with their vision, their passion, and their business smarts. Not only that, but I saw how we could work together to advance our shared vision for better buildings. Not long after, WELL became GBCI's first client besides LEED, and together we're already making a world of difference.

I know what you're probably thinking: *That's a lot of acronyms, Rick, and I don't really understand how they're saving the planet* . . .

I hear you! After all, how could an environmental nonprofit create a massive global marketplace and, in doing so, drive profit, innovation, and impact across the largest asset class in the world? How could one little rating system seed such a massive movement? Sounds pretty farfetched, right? I'll admit—it still amazes me, too.

But once you understand *how* LEED works, you'll understand *why* it works.

BUILDING GREEN

"You never change things by fighting the existing reality. To change something, build a new model that makes the existing model obsolete."
—*Buckminster Fuller*

THEY SAY A PICTURE IS WORTH A THOUSAND WORDS, but this one is worth a whole lot more.

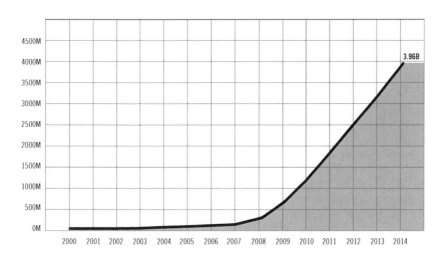

Can you guess what is growing so fast?

No, it's not iPhones sales, the national debt, the population of China, or the number of hits for the most popular cat video on YouTube. It's the number of square feet of LEED-certified real estate worldwide. This chart shows, plain and simple, how big and how fast the green building industry has grown in just the past fifteen years. And this is only the beginning. By 2018, the green building industry in the U.S. alone is expected to nearly double in size.

You might be wondering: *What's making the green building industry scale like this?* But if you've read this far, you already know the answer.

More than 80 Fortune 100 companies use LEED certification to drive down costs and increase profits. Their buildings make skylines and headlines, with names you'll recognize. The Bank of America Tower in midtown Manhattan, the fifth-tallest building in the United States, is LEED Platinum. In 2014, Starbucks—one of the world's most admired companies (and one of mine, too)—opened its 500th LEED-certified location. There's even a LEED-certified NFL stadium: Soldier Field, home of the Chicago Bears. I've had the privilege of awarding LEED plaques to green buildings all around the world, from PepsiCo factories in Shanghai to the original Guinness Brewery at St. James's Gate in Dublin to my local elementary school in Syracuse.

As LEED continues to grow, real estate investors around the world are recognizing the value of having green buildings in their portfolios. Researchers have found that real estate investment trusts (REITs) perform better when their portfolios include LEED-certified properties. That's one reason why, while the U.S. construction market was badly hurting in the depths of the Great Recession, the green building sector actually expanded.

No, green building isn't taking off because the marketplace suddenly grew an environmental conscience. It's growing because of the *profits* associated with building green. Should we be upset by that? Should it trouble us that the people holding the purse strings seem to care more about cost savings than about environmental stewardship or human health? I bet that fact makes a lot of environmentalists uncomfortable. Actually, I know it does.

But it doesn't bother me. Not one bit.

Given the outsized environmental and human impact of buildings, regardless of motive, the tremendous growth of LEED is doing enormous good. According to the United Nations Environment Programme, buildings account for 40 percent of worldwide energy consumption and up to one-third of greenhouse gas emissions. Rating systems like LEED, and those it has inspired in countries around the world, are directly mitigating one of the largest contributors to climate change. But they're doing more than that. *They're improving people's lives in real and tangible ways.* And that's why we shouldn't cringe at the profits associated with building green—we should celebrate them. In fact, the financial benefits of green building are not only compatible with positive environmental and human health outcomes—they are the driving them.

———

Let me preface the below by saying that the health care industry is amazing, and its professionals—doctors, nurses, and EMTs—are true heroes. That being said, I have to be honest: I hate hospitals. In my experience, they're dimly lit places with vinyl curtains, terrible smells, and corridors that are as depressing as they are sterile—yes, in the clean way, but also in the get-me-the-hell-out-of-here way. So when I first set foot in Dell Children's Medical Center in Austin, Texas, it was with a fair amount of trepidation—and not only about the building, but also about the people I would encounter inside. Dell Children's, which is owned and operated by Seton Healthcare Family, a health ministry of Ascension Health, is a place where ailing children go to receive treatment for cancer and other life-threatening diseases. Tragically, some never leave. As the father of two grown kids, my heart breaks at the thought of any child suffering from a severe illness.

But when I stepped into Dell Children's, all of my anxieties melted away. The whole facility is filled with light, color, art, and the sounds of water and, yes, even laughter. I got to walk around and see the beautiful healing gardens and courtyards, and to breathe the fresh, clean indoor air. And let me tell you something: it smells *good*. For a moment,

I completely forgot that I was in a hospital. I was simply in a gorgeous building that seemed full of happiness and hope. Most hospitals I've been in feel like places you go to die, but Dell Children's is a building that screams life at the top of its lungs. That's why it's one of my favorite LEED buildings in the entire world.

Dell Children's Medical Center made history in 2008 when it became the first hospital ever certified as LEED Platinum. Then, in 2013, after adding the W. H. and Elaine McCarty South Tower, it made history again by becoming the first hospital certified as LEED Platinum *twice* (this time under USGBC's LEED for Healthcare rating system). There are tremendous environmental benefits associated with that level of certification. Between its landscaping, which features local Texas plants that require less water, and its efficient plumbing fixtures, the hospital saves 3.1 million gallons of water every year. Eighty percent of the building is lit naturally. And the hospital saves enough energy from its efficient lights and air-conditioning to power 300 homes.

These are impressive statistics. But while we often talk about green buildings as being environmentally friendly, the more notable characteristic of a LEED building is that it's human friendly. And Dell Children's might be one of the most human-friendly buildings ever constructed.

For one thing, the building is good to the staff. Dell Children's has an exceptionally low turnover rate. There's no question that the hospital management is top-notch, that Austin is one of the most livable cities in America, and that working with kids is one of the most fulfilling things you can do with your life. I'm sure that's all part of it. But a 2014 study that looked closely at data from the five years before and after Dell Children's LEED certification found that, compared with the previous non-LEED hospital, staff turnover at the new Dell Children's was down by more than 6.5 percent. I'm almost positive it's not because of the low-flow toilets. Thanks to the natural light, the quality of the air, and the aesthetics of the building that make you feel happier and more alert, people *want* to work there. And because the hospital's employees are so happy at their jobs, hospital administrators don't have to spend time and money to recruit and train new workers.

But the staff members at Dell Children's aren't just happier. They're also healthier. The same 2014 study found that, compared with the old hospital, staff injuries and illnesses were down by 7 percent. You might argue that these positive effects are not because of LEED, but simply because the building is brand-new. But data from the other new, non-LEED hospitals in the same network revealed that workplace illnesses and injuries were still 3 percent lower at Dell Children's.

Dell Children's is an incredible example of how a building can transform the lives of the people who live and work inside of it. But what amazes me even more than the quantifiable effects it has on its staff is the qualitative impact the building has on its patients and their families.

When I went to visit Dell Children's, the hospital administrator told me an incredible story. A young boy—I'll call him Johnny—was a patient receiving chemotherapy at the hospital for about six months. His parents visited him every day, and when Johnny had the energy, his favorite thing to do with his mom and dad was not to play a board game or turn on the television; it was to show them all the different parts of the building that he loved. Eventually Johnny was well enough to go home. But amazingly, he didn't want to leave the hospital!

We shouldn't be surprised by stories like this. As early as 1984, Roger Urlich compared patients who, after their surgery, looked out their windows onto either a brick wall or a group of trees. It turns out, according to Urlich, "patients with window views of the trees spent less time in the hospital than those with views of the brick wall." Finally, thanks to LEED, our buildings are catching up to this important research.

The health care implications of green building couldn't be more exciting. Imagine a world in which patients feel better and are treated by nurses and doctors who feel better, too. Imagine a world in which patients are happier and heal faster in their hospital rooms—and are able to leave those rooms a day or two earlier. One of the things that will help make this vision a reality is the emerging trend of biophilic design. By paying attention to things like allowing natural light, offering a view of nature, and using the built environment to connect us to the natural world, we can significantly reduce stress and even improve medical outcomes. It's the reason USGBC offers a LEED pilot credit for biophilia—and the reason so many architects and designers are getting on board.

The benefits to human beings of green hospitals are clear. But so are the financial benefits, given our incredibly expensive health care system. Recall that Dell Children's green facility has 6.5 percent lower staff turnover. Compared with the hospital it replaced, that 2014 study found Dell Children's saves more than $2.17 million every year simply by *not* turning over its employees. And what's more, Dell Children's even has a lower turnover rate, and lower associated costs, than other new, non-LEED hospitals.

At the same time, we know workplace illnesses and injuries are down by 7 percent at Dell Children's, and while that might not seem like a lot, it is when you consider that decline translated into $4.5 million in savings for the new Dell Children's compared with the original facility. And once again, according to the study, Dell Children's also saves significantly in this area when compared with non-LEED hospitals in the same network.

And that's just the savings Dell Children's achieves on its personnel. Just think about the savings when it comes to its patients. According to the Kaiser Family Foundation, the estimated average cost to a hospital for one day of patient care is $2,157. Imagine the days of patient care you could eliminate across the country just by admitting patients to hospitals that feature natural light, clean air, and a view to nature. The cost savings would run quickly into the billions.

I'm not a doctor, but I know that better buildings make people better, too. They help us work better. They help us heal better. And that's why more and more people feel better about investing in green buildings—because they can see the financial *and* the human benefits for everyone involved.

In fact, green buildings can benefit entire communities. Just ask the residents of Lake Mills, Wisconsin.

Faced with aging, unsafe, ill-equipped, overcrowded schools, the Lake Mills Area School District knew it needed to do something. Six times the district tried to pass referendums to secure the funding needed to improve its middle school, and six times it failed. The voters had said no, over and over again, to measures that would increase their property taxes in order to pay for facility upgrades and enhancements of any kind. Saddled with a crumbling, dilapidated school that had reached the end of its useful life, the district had to try a different approach to convince taxpayers to make the necessary investment. So the district's leaders engaged Miron Construction Co. Inc., one of Wisconsin's largest construction firms, to assist in crafting a plan that would gain community support and ultimately pass a referendum.

To give the public an up-close-and-personal understanding of the situation, the district and Miron took members of the community on a tour of the existing middle school building to show them just how bad it really was. They saw the sixty-year-old boiler and the frayed electrical wiring for the light fixtures. They felt the lack of air-conditioning and daylight and the poor indoor air quality. Despite the offer, no one wanted to walk through the nearly 70-year-old underground tunnel to get from the middle school to the gymnasium. The tour pointed out an obvious truth: in order to protect the health and safety of the students, the community needed a new school.

Miron and the district then surveyed the community—in person and online—in an attempt to understand taxpayers' concerns and needs. It turns out, one of the community's top goals was sustainability. That's when Theresa Lehman, the director of sustainable services at Miron—a dear friend of mine and a fiercely committed champion of green buildings—got involved. Theresa and the district leaders began working to integrate specifically defined sustainability goals into the design process for the new school, using the LEED for Schools rating system as a framework. They never identified LEED as a goal—they simply set out to make the school as sustainable as possible given the budget they had to work with. But they soon discovered that choosing sustainability does not necessarily mean spending more money.

In November 2007, on the seventh try, voters finally approved a $15.5 million referendum to renovate and expand the existing middle school, with one exception: the community wanted to keep the old 1938 gymnasium, which was—as gyms often are—full of fond memories of pep rallies, basketball games, and the sort of things we get sentimental about when we think back on our childhood.

The new Lake Mills Middle School (along with the old gymnasium) opened its doors in the fall of 2010. In the months that followed, it was officially recognized as the first LEED Platinum public K–12 school in America and was named "the world's greenest school" by USGBC's Center for Green Schools. And while that's certainly a point of pride, the people of Lake Mills had another reason to celebrate. Thanks to the district's desire to establish sustainable goals from the start, and the team's commitment to executing those goals, the project's final cost was only $14.8 million, enabling the taxpayers to *recoup* $750,000 before the school ever opened. What's more, the middle school continues to perform better than expected, saving taxpayers more than $85,000 a year on energy compared with a typical code-compliant school— thanks to the geothermal heating and cooling system, the high-performance lighting, and a better building envelope. In fact, when the community realized its entire brand-new green school used less energy than the old 1938 gymnasium *alone*, their sentimentality morphed into sustainability, and the gym was torn down!

Renovating and expanding a middle school for the same cost as a non-green, code-compliant school is a terrific achievement. But what happened next speaks to the power of green buildings to inspire and spark change.

On the heels of the successful completion of the middle school, the Lake Mills School District turned its attention to the elementary school, which was built in 1964. It was déjà vu all over again. The building was in worse shape than the old middle school; it was severely overcrowded, with a leaky roof, a boiler on its last legs, and walls contaminated with asbestos and lead.

But this time the district leaders proposed something radical: a new elementary school that would be even greener than the middle school. That's right—greener than the award-winning, LEED Platinum, greenest school in the world. When Theresa was asked point-blank if she could make this happen, her response was, "Hell, yeah!"

Now, the community was not ecstatic about the possibility of another tax increase. But something was different this time. They understood the benefits that resulted from a high-performance, healthy learning environment. When the district surveyed residents about the idea of deconstructing the old Prospect Elementary and building a new elementary school, one respondent said, "We have already seen how the middle school saves money on heating costs, so it seems like an obvious financial and moral decision to build a school that will be best for the environment."

The Lake Mills Middle School had opened the eyes and hearts of the community to the benefits of green building. According to Dean Sanders, the district administrator, students and staff in the middle school—even his own son—have reported "significantly reduced respiratory illnesses and no longer need to take asthma or allergy medication." The shop teacher, who had been taking five or six doses of allergy medication every day for the past twenty years while teaching in the old building, was off all of his medication within two weeks of being in the newly renovated building. Not only did the students become more engaged in the learning process, but staff and parents alike began to notice how the children took ownership of their new school.

And so, for the first time in the history of the school district, the referendum to build a new green elementary school was passed on the very first vote.

To be clear, Lake Mills is not a liberal haven. It's a small, rural, conservative community in Jefferson County, thirty-five miles east of Madison, Wisconsin. The same year the people of Lake Mills voted to build a new sustainable elementary school, Mitt Romney won Jefferson County with 53 percent of the vote. I mention this only because the decision these voters made was "financial and moral" but not political. To me, this is evidence that voting red or blue doesn't change the inherent value of building green. In all honesty, it goes to show that education is key—in every sense of the term. As Theresa likes to say, "When people are well-informed, they will make well-informed decisions."

The decision to build green was a very good one indeed for the Lake Mills School District. While the original referendum approved $18.7 million for the elementary school project, the facility came in $400,000 under budget. But the cost savings doesn't end there. The new school features a 10 kW photovoltaic system, a solar thermal hot-water system, a vegetated green roof, high-performance dimming LED light fixtures, daylighting controls, low-flow plumbing fixtures, ENERGY STAR kitchen appliances, and a geo-thermal heating and cooling system. All this results in a 50 percent energy reduction compared with a code-compliant school, saving the community $131,000 in energy costs—*each year*.

Even a first grader can see that's some pretty compelling math. But for the Lake Mills School District, just like at Dell Children's, quantifiable financial benefits have incalculable human benefits. The air quality inside the new elementary school is so high that during the first year of operation, Principal Amanda Thompson recorded a 75 percent reduction in asthma- and allergy-related incidents compared with the final year of operation at the old elementary school. The school is also seeing fewer absences by both students and staff. The classroom acoustics at Lake Mills Elementary School are so good that teachers no longer have to yell, and students sitting in the back can hear loud and clear. And everyone loves the abundance of natural daylight.

When I finally got a chance to visit the Lake Mills Elementary School, I saw firsthand what the community was so excited about. When you walk in, you feel energized and alert. You immediately appreciate how the green features of the building—from the construction materials used to the air you breathe—contribute to a better learning experience. In fact, every person you meet in the town of Lake Mills seems to understand the myriad benefits of green buildings. And that's the real promise of green schools. The students who learn there each and every day—the next generation of future leaders in business, politics, science, education, and technology—intuitively get the impact and value of sustainability. People are products of their environment, so simply by educating students in green buildings, we are seeding a movement that will last longer and spread farther than you or I could imagine.

You might say, "Sure, Rick, hospitals and schools—anything with kids, really—make green building seem like a logical investment. But what about something more out of left field?"

OK, then—how about something *literally* out of left field?

Baseball has long been America's pastime. Ever since 1846, when the Knickerbockers played the very first game, the sport has grown to capture fans all around the world. And yet it feels as though the only time we talk about "green" in the context of baseball is in reference to the Green Monster at Fenway Park. The only mentions of "performance enhancement" have to do with the latest violation of Major League Baseball's doping policy.

But when the Miami Marlins and the people of Miami invested in a new ballpark, they were interested in a very different kind of performance enhancement and a few different shades of green. In fact, one of the first things the county, the city, and the ownership agreed on was that the new ballpark had to be LEED Silver. But thanks to their early and focused commitment to sustainability—from the Marlins organization to the architect to the construction company—Marlins Park became the first LEED *Gold*-certified professional sports facility with a retractable roof.

Sustainability is a team sport, and the Marlins had an all-star roster. But to fully understand the scale of their achievement, let's take a step back and consider the environmental impact of a ballpark.

In a 162-game season, you've got eighty-one home games. That's eighty-one games where tens of thousands of people get in their cars and drive to the ballpark. Factor in that many of these games are at night, which means you've got to turn on the big lights (in addition to all the regular lights and the screens large and small). On top of that, remember that in places like Miami, where during the height of the season temperatures can regularly reach into the nineties, air-conditioning becomes necessary. If you think it's expensive to keep your house cool, imagine trying to cool the house that Ruth built—or in this case, the 928,000 square feet of Marlins Park.

The environmental impact of a baseball venue is already enormous—and we haven't even thrown out the first pitch!

Now, think for a moment about what those tens of thousands of people do *inside* the stadium. You've got thousands of hot dogs grilling, thousands of beers being poured, and thousands of people buying peanuts and crackerjacks—after which the maintenance staff has to *root root root* through thousands of pounds of trash. Then add to the equation all the delivery trucks restocking the concession stands and the garbage trucks hauling away the refuse. By the time you get to the seventh-inning stretch, fans have flushed hundreds of toilets countless times. And that's to say nothing of watering the outfield.

Multiply all this by the thirty teams, and we've got a major-league problem.

While you may watch baseball in appreciation of all the utility infielders, baseball stadiums are all about utility *bills.* They're incredibly resource intensive—which means they're also an incredible opportunity to become more efficient. You've heard of *Moneyball,* now let's talk "Greenball"—the Miami Marlins and their LEED Gold ballpark.

Marlins Park uses 22.4 percent less energy than other buildings its size, which translates to roughly $500,000 a year in savings. On top of that, the ballpark uses half as much water as a similar stadium, with the waterless urinals alone reducing water consumption by six million gallons every year. So while the team had a 208–278 win–loss record from 2012 to 2014—which, honestly, is not great—its environmental record has been a home run.

On my tour of the ballpark, I was impressed to see all these features put to work in such a beautiful facility. They are a tremendous testament to the Marlins organization's continued commitment to sustainable operations. But there's more. In the 2014 season, the Marlins recycling stats were just incredible:

The organization recycled 51 percent of its waste, bringing the Marlins' career totals up to 52 tons of oil and 92 tons of cardboard saved. The Marlins even recycled the sod and garden waste after redoing the field—780 tons, to be precise. (Talk about home field advantage!) In 2014, the team also donated more than 10,000 meals to a local senior center instead of allowing leftover food to go to waste. The floors of the clubhouses are made from recycled Nike shoes. And my favorite fact: it only costs $10 in electricity to open the 8,000 tons of steel that make up the retractable roof. That's less than a beer and a hot dog cost at a ballgame!

That said, the beer is doing its part, too. One of the more amazing things I saw during my tour of the ballpark was the centralized beer distribution system. Instead of running kegs up and down to every concession stand on every level, tubes throughout the building bring the beer up into the taps. From an efficiency and safety standpoint, this makes perfect sense. But from a sustainability standpoint, it's the kind of benefit that's hard to measure but easy to see. If you're moving and cooling fewer kegs, you're using less energy; if you're only filling up three large tanks instead of constantly restocking hundreds of kegs, you're bringing in fewer trucks.

Marlins Park—from the taps to the retractable roof—proves there is literally no ceiling to what we can do when it comes to greening sports facilities. And not just baseball stadiums. On a trip to Brazil in 2012, I met with leaders of the country's largest pension fund. At that meeting, I was told that the fund had decided to invest only in green-rated buildings, starting with venues for the 2014 FIFA World Cup and the 2016 Olympic Games. This is huge—but it also confirms the trend. Ultimately, whether it's Marlins Park or an Olympic stadium, it should be clear by now that building green is a win-win-win. It's a win for people, it's a win for the planet, and for those of you keeping score, it's a win for the bottom line, too.

Along with all the benefits already mentioned, a sports stadium offers one of the most important stages in the world, particularly from a child's perspective. Our kids see athletes as heroes, and what our heroes do, we emulate. In order to be like them, we learn and we advance. Just as our athletes continue to inspire and teach our children values such as hard work and perseverance, sports stadiums are a tremendous opportunity to set the right public example and educate an adoring, young public. If we truly want to inspire a generation of sustainability leaders, we have to meet our kids where they are—and meet our culture where it is. We have to establish greenthink not as an elusive ideal, but as a (dare I say?) fun and ubiquitous aspect of everyday life.

Not long ago, I traveled to Mumbai, India, to visit the city's first LEED Platinum building. It's a beautiful structure that resembles many LEED buildings around the world, including those highlighted in this chapter. You can see the use of glass to let in natural light . . . the LED fixtures on each of the floors . . . all the sustainable features that, by now, we've come to expect from green buildings.

And yet as soon as you step outside, it's a very different story. As far as the eye can see, in every direction, there are slums. I saw people who have only a piece of cardboard—or, if they're lucky, a sheet of corrugated metal—protecting them from the elements. The smell of human waste and trash hit me in waves alongside the oppressive heat. I remember, standing outside this space-age tower juxtaposed with the Stone Age shantytown surrounding it, feeling as though I had landed on another planet.

This juxtaposition is tragically common. From the favelas of São Paolo to disadvantaged communities in the Bronx, poverty and desolation are often found not very far from gleaming new LEED buildings. On the way back to my hotel in Mumbai, I kept thinking about these stark contrasts, and honestly, it made me really uncomfortable. While LEED addresses the problem of unsustainable buildings, buildings only partially address the problem of our unsustainable and unjust global society.

Don't get me wrong. LEED is fantastic—for profits, for the planet, and for people all around the world. And while those first two are important, for me sustainability has always been about people. Green buildings allow us to live better, to work better, to heal and learn and play better. But in world in which environmental degradation is severely impacting—and in some cases, ending—people's lives, you have to stop and ask: What more can we do to make the world better, safer, healthier, fairer, happier, and yes, more sustainable?

To me, the answer is obvious. We have to take the principles of LEED and extend them far beyond the four walls of a building, out to the four corners of the world itself. We must take the lessons of LEED and use them—urgently—to improve not just our built environment, but also our social institutions, our political institutions, and the very fabric of our society at large.

This chapter is filled with a lot of firsts. The first LEED Platinum school. The first LEED Platinum hospital. The first LEED Gold ballpark with a retractable roof. My money—and a lot of other people's—is betting on the fact that soon we won't be talking about the first LEED Platinum building in this industry or that town. We'll be talking about the first LEED certified *city*.

If you think that's far-fetched, consider the pace of change and development in emerging economies around the world. In China, whole new cities are springing up practically overnight. According to McKinsey & Company, "70 to 80 percent of the India of 2030 is yet to be built." But it will be. And if the gorgeous LEED building I toured in Mumbai is any indication, it will be sustainable. Just think of all the hospitals and homes, the stadiums and schools that can improve the lives of billions of people living in the developing world.

This is not a fantasy. The environmental benefits of green-think are undeniable. The human benefits cannot be under-stated. And the profit motive—the ability to save and even *make* money while saving the environment and saving lives—continues to drive companies and communities toward higher standards of efficiency and sustainability. Experts and econo-mists, corporate and civil society leaders all around the world are getting wise to the incredible power of sustainability—and rising to the challenge of doing for our world what LEED is doing for buildings.

From where I'm standing, it is no longer a question of *if* we will see a sustainable world. The green building movement has proved that we have the ability and the global demand to drive this change. The only variable is *when*. When will greenthink become second nature? When will some people get their heads out of the unsustainable, unprofitable sands? To be fair, I don't know how soon we'll see a LEED-certified city—though it's likely sooner than you'd think—but I do know that if we keep building on this work, and keep build-ing green, we will continue to see extraordinary growth in LEED and unprecedented social and environmental benefits as a result.

Ultimately, to be truly sustainable, we have to pull in eco-nomics and politics and food sourcing and transportation and manufacturing and every other sector and discipline there is, until we have a fully three-dimensional view of sus-tainability. The stories of the green buildings in this chapter are among my very favorite. But even so, they're merely foot-notes in a larger, epic sustainability story that's being written all around us.

ECO-NOMICS

"The throwing out of balance of the
resources of Nature throws out of balance
*also the lives of men."**
—*Franklin Delano Roosevelt*

THERE'S A FAMOUS *RYOKAN*—a small Japanese inn—called Houshi, situated atop a hot spring about two hundred miles east of Tokyo. Founded in the year 718 (not a typo!), and managed by the same family for forty-six consecutive generations, Houshi is among the oldest businesses in the world. And for more than a millennium, it has been guided by the same mantra, perhaps the world's oldest corporate mission statement: "Take care of fire, learn from water, cooperate with nature."

Cooperate with nature.

Thirteen hundred years later, the biggest and most powerful

---

* And women!

corporations on Earth are beginning to understand that this is more than just a long-lived tagline for one *ryokan*. It's the single most important business strategy of the twenty-first century.

Market forces are beginning to push companies to conserve resources and adopt sustainable business practices. As a result, they're generating more profits, attracting more customers, and inspiring a greater degree of brand loyalty than their competitors—and the stocks of sustainable enterprises are outperforming the market, too. So while some companies are getting ahead of the sustainability curve, others are in for a rude awakening as conventional economic wisdom is upended and environmental factors begin to make or break businesses, industries, and even entire economies.

It's no exaggeration to say that the traditional understanding of economic growth—what enables it, what encourages it, and what threatens it—needs to be completely overhauled. So let's start from the very beginning: the founding of economics as science, nearly 240 years ago.

In the beginning, of course, there was Adam. Adam Smith, that is. He wasn't from the Bible, but he did write one, of sorts. In 1776, the same year Thomas Jefferson penned the Declaration of Independence, Smith wrote his own founding document: *An Inquiry into the Nature and Causes of the Wealth of Nations,* which created an entirely new field of thought.

You might remember some of Smith's ideas. (Or maybe you learned and then forgot them by your sophomore year of college.) The invisible hand. Absolute advantage. Real and nominal price. Smith wrote about all these concepts, and he also had something to say about the economics of the environment.

Smith wrote, "The word *VALUE* ... has two different meanings." One, he noted, "expresses the utility of some particular object." The other is the ability of an object to be exchanged for goods. "The things which have the greatest value in use," Smith argued, "have frequently little or no value in exchange." In other words, they can't be bartered with or spent as currency. Smith even used an environmental example: "Nothing is more useful than water; but it will purchase scarce anything; scarce anything can be had in exchange for it."

What economies value instead is nature *transformed*. The market does put a price on *some* of nature's bounty in its original form—for instance, natural gas straight from the ground, crude oil straight from the well, grapes straight from the vine. But the economic importance of most natural resources is that they can be turned into far more precious products. Natural gas is worth a lot more when burned to generate electricity. Crude is worth a lot more when converted into gasoline. Grapes are worth a lot more when they're turned into a nice chardonnay.

I'm no economist, but if you ask me, it's pretty clear the entire premise of economic growth up until now has been based on this idea of transformation. And transformation, it's worth pointing out, is the very opposite of conservation. The more you transform—the more natural resources you convert into products for the marketplace—the more wealth you create.

In his excellent history of the environmental movement,

A Fierce Green Fire, Phillip Shabecoff tells the story of the timber industry and its impact. Two hundred years ago, the United States was blanketed with dense forests, and timber was quickly becoming one of the nation's largest and most lucrative industries. In response to the demand for more wood, lumberjacks moved across the nation with their axes and saws. They chopped down forests from New England to the Pacific Northwest. At every turn, timber tycoons left behind them deforested habitats that flooded worse and more often than before. Some turned into swamps. As Schabecoff writes, "Soil erosion, loss of watersheds, and disappearance of game had by the latter part of the nineteenth century become national problems as the once seemingly endless forests were methodically leveled."

From an economic perspective, of course, this environmental devastation was well worth it. After all, timber was being transformed into ships, shops, homes, barns, mills, looms, pianos, paper, factories, furniture, railroad ties, and barrels for aging whiskey—and jobs. Lumber was building a nation and creating unprecedented wealth.

Turning nature into wealth. Two and a half centuries later, that's still how most of us think about the economy. But things are starting to change.

Like me, Mark Tercek is an executive-turned-environmentalist. A former managing director and partner at Goldman Sachs, he's now the president and CEO of the Nature Conservancy, a leading global environmental organization. Mark, along with author Jonathan Adams, put out a fabulous book called *Nature's Fortune,* which explores the importance of understanding and investing in what he calls "natural capital." Tercek argues that nature has value *independent* of transformation:

> For generations, economists assumed that manufacturers could run down natural capital as much as they wanted, so long as the economy overall created enough man-made capital to replace it. When the scale of economic activity remained small in comparison to the scale of the planet itself, this may have been a workable assumption—but not anymore.

Tercek is right. It's pretty clear to me (and to countless other environmentalists and capitalists who have come to this conclusion) that Adam Smith's classical theory—that many of nature's goods have little to no value in exchange—was based on surplus. And from a global perspective, for a very, very long time there indeed has been a surplus of water, trees, minerals, and every natural resource we could think to put to use. We had all these things in endless abundance, in fact, for the first 10,000 years or so of human civilization.

Then population growth picked up. As we made progress in industry, medicine, agriculture, and sanitation, humans began to lead longer, healthier lives. In 1804, the world's population hit the historic one billion mark. By 1927, that figure had doubled. By 1974, it had doubled again. In 1987, the population topped five billion people—having climbed by three billion in the course of just sixty years—and then, in October 1999, UN Secretary-General Kofi Annan greeted the world's six billionth person in a hospital in Sarajevo. Only twelve years after that, in 2011, another baby, this time in the Philippines, was named the seventh billionth human.

And as the world's population has grown exponentially, so has its consumption. According to the United Nations Environment Programme, consumption of construction minerals in Asia and the Pacific region has already increased twelve times its level in 1970. Utilization of metal ores and industrial materials has increased 800 percent. In fact, certain patterns of consumption have grown *faster* than the overall population. Today, water use is climbing at double the rate of population growth. According to the Food and Agriculture Organization of the United Nations, in 1961, humans consumed about seventy million tons of meat. Nowadays we have twice the number of people, but we consume four times as much meat! It's worth noting here that livestock produce not just meat and manure, but also heat-trapping greenhouse gases like methane and nitrous oxide—a major reason why agriculture accounted for 7.7 percent of all U.S. greenhouse gas emissions in 2013.

This isn't an indictment of consumerism—or carnivorism. I'm a big fan of New York strips and California cabernets. But when several billion more people start loving these things, too—and, more to the point, when they start being able to afford them—then we have to start thinking differently about the environment and the economy. Put it this way: according to science writer Tim De Chant and data from the Global Footprint Network, if all the world's people lived like Americans, we'd need more than four Earths' worth of land to sustain ourselves.

Well, we don't have four Earths. We barely have one anymore.

Today, humanity is putting in an order for natural resources that Mother Nature simply cannot fill. By 2030, the global middle class is expected to swell from 1.8 billion to 4.9 billion people. According to the consulting firm Ernst & Young, China's middle class alone may number a billion consumers. It isn't hard to see what will happen—what is *already* happening.

It all goes back to the "tragedy of the commons," a concept popularized in 1968 by ecologist Garrett Hardin. In his famous essay in the journal *Science,* Hardin described a nineteenth-century analogy for population growth in which farmers were allowed to graze their livestock for free on common land. The arrangement worked just fine, so long as there was enough grass for every cow. The problem arose when the livestock reached a critical mass—when there was just enough grass to feed them all. At that point, grazing any more livestock would begin to damage the pasture. The cattle would overfeed. The grass would turn to mud. The field would turn fallow.

Each farmer understood this. But each also made a calculation: If he *did* graze an additional cow, he *alone* would reap the benefit. The cost of the damage to the pasture, however, would be divided among *all* the farmers. According to Hardin, the only "sensible course for him to pursue is to add another animal to his herd. And then another; and another . . ." And that was the tragedy: the farmers' sensible, short-term economic decisions would lead them to destroy the pasture—and therefore their livelihoods—in the long run.

For Hardin, this devastated pasture was the perfect metaphor for the planet. Nearly half a century later, it still is. Hardin's concerns about overpopulation have proved more accurate than he could have imagined. Today, we're consuming larger and larger quantities of the world's "commons." We haven't just grazed the Earth—we've *razed* it. We've dug it up, drilled into it, strip-mined it, and cut it down. In the short term, these actions are economically sensible for individual people, corporations, and nations. Like the farmers, however, we've reached a tipping point where "overgrazing" is beginning to destroy our land and our livelihoods.

There is a wealth of data to back this up. A group called the Natural Capital Coalition (formerly, TEEB for Business Coalition) published a study to explore the top one hundred ways the private sector is impacting the environment, from water pollution to greenhouse gas emissions. These externalities, the study found, are costing society $4.7 *trillion* each year. In fact, according to Principles for Responsible Investment and the UNEP Finance Initiative, the world's three thousand largest companies alone wreaked $2.15 trillion in environmental havoc in 2008.

And now, industry is starting to bear the economic cost of climate change. During 2012, ongoing droughts and heat afflicting much of the United States resulted in staggering amounts of lost crops for the U.S. farm industry and cost the Federal Crop Insurance Corporation $17.3 billion—a record amount. In 2014, California's drought alone cost the agriculture sector there $2.2 billion. The monthlong blaze that engulfed Bastrop, Texas, in September 2011 consumed nearly 1,700 businesses and homes and resulted in $360 million in damages. It was the most destructive—and most expensive—wildfire in the state's history. That same year, when halfway around the world flooding ravaged Thailand, Intel alone estimated a $1 billion hit in revenues thanks to the resulting shortage of hard disk drives. Sony and Honda also faced flooding-related production problems that contributed to a 2.3 percent decline of the Japanese economy in the fourth quarter of 2011.

And then there was 2012's Hurricane Sandy, which, in addition to taking the lives of more than one hundred people in the northeast U.S., destroyed tens of billions of dollars in personal property and infrastructure. We saw the devastation in terrifying high definition on the news. What the newsreel didn't capture, however, was the accompanying private-sector devastation. It's estimated that, in the U.S. alone, the storm caused at least $20 billion in lost economic activity and business interruption—workers who couldn't work, shoppers who couldn't shop, and commerce that ground to a halt in Sandy's wake.

The National Weather Service measures hurricanes in categories 1 through 5, but the private sector measures them in dollars and cents. As you think back over the past decade and add up all the losses from Hurricanes Rita, Katrina, and Sandy, and from the dozens of other extreme weather events—tornadoes, flooding, wildfires, droughts, epic blizzards—an important question comes to mind:

Who the heck is paying for all this?

The answer is, the insurance industry—a $4.6 trillion sector that makes up 7 percent of the global economy.

As the journal *Science* reported, insurance claims related to weather catastrophes "have more than doubled each decade since the 1980s, adjusted for inflation." The Insurance Information Institute notes that eight of the ten most expensive hurricanes in U.S. history have all hit since 2004. All indications are that this trend will only continue. According to PricewaterhouseCoopers (PwC), "Between 1990 and 2009, hurricanes and tropical storms accounted for 45.2 percent of total catastrophe losses, and the rate and intensity of these storms is predicted to increase with global climate change." Big storms, meanwhile, aren't the only big concern for the insurance industry. As PwC notes, "In addition to catastrophic events, insurers must also consider man-made degradation of the environment."

All this explains the frayed nerves of J. Eric Smith, CEO of the major reinsurer Swiss Re Americas, who told *Time* magazine, "We see the long-term effect of climate change on society, and it really frightens us."

Jack Ehnes, CEO of the California State Teachers' Retirement System—a 870,000-member pension fund—once called insurance "the oxygen that keeps our economy alive." Today, environmental degradation is not only polluting the air we breathe and altering the climate of our planet—it's starting to suck the air out of the lungs of the private sector.

To use another phrase economists like, *there's no free lunch*. The environmental disasters we've taken for granted are starting to catch up with us, and paying for these losses and other externalities is threatening the very foundation of our global economy.

———

In December 1971, Harvard professor Simon Kuznets traveled to Stockholm to collect an award he'd won—the Nobel Prize in Economic Sciences. Kuznets was the first to observe that as economics develop—as industrialization occurs and incomes rise—inequality grows, too. Initially, at least. At some point, according to Kuznets, the trend reverses. Then, the creation of wealth becomes a force for good, breeding economic equality and a large middle class. This phenomenon has become known as "the Kuznets curve."

Kuznets passed away in 1985. But in 1991, two other economists noticed that a similar curve applied to a different area of concern: environmental degradation. Gene Grossman and Alan Krueger found that in certain cases, and in certain places, the relationship between economic development and inequality is similar to the relationship between economic development and pollution. At first, rising incomes damage the environment. But then the trend reverses, and more wealth coincides with more conservation.

For two decades, this compelling theory—"the environmental Kuznets curve"—has continued to elicit intellectual debate and further study about whether economic growth does indeed lead to environmental stability. Some of the controversy stems from the fact that this relationship is clearer for some pollutants—such as sulfur dioxide, which Grossman and Krueger initially studied. For others, the data is simply not available. And, as is common with these kinds of studies, it's not always the case that correlation implies causation.

Despite all the uncertainty, I do believe that there is a positive relationship between economies and environments. I just think that most economists don't see the whole picture: It's not just that more wealth leads to sustainability. *Sustainability also leads to more wealth.*

In 2015, investment firm Morgan Stanley issued a landmark report titled "Sustainable Investing's Performance Potential." In the past, the report noted, investors have been leery of putting their money behind companies that adopt strong environmental, social, and governance (ESG) policies, fearing that such progressive businesses would fare worse in the marketplace. But Morgan Stanley's more recent analysis upends that outdated conventional wisdom.

The report analyzed the market performance over a seven-year period of 10,228 mutual funds and 2,874 separately managed accounts. The results are incredible—but not surprising (to me, at least). According to Morgan Stanley, "Investing in sustainability has usually met, and often exceeded, the performance of comparable traditional investments." For instance, funds focused on sustainability "met or exceeded the median return of traditional equity funds for 64 percent of the time periods examined." And from 2008 to 2014, "sustainable equity funds met or exceeded median returns for five out of six different equity classes examined, for example, large-cap growth."

It turns out that investing in sustainability has long been a winning strategy—for the past twenty-five years, in fact! According to Morgan Stanley, "long-term annual returns of the MSCI KLD 400 Social Index, which comprises firms scoring highly on environmental, social, and governance criteria, outperformed the S&P 500, a benchmark of the broader U.S. stock market, by 45 basis points, since its inception in 1990." It's no wonder Morgan Stanley's Institute for Sustainable Investing concludes that adopting ESG is a smart strategy for investors. And investors are catching on. According to Morgan Stanley:

> A growing number of investors are exploring sustainable investing. In 2012, $1 out of every $9 of US assets under professional management was invested in some form of sustainable investment, primarily in public equities. In 2014 that number increased to $1 out of every $6—to a total of $6.57 trillion now invested sustainably.

The environment may not have a ticker symbol or be listed on any stock exchange. As companies around the world are starting to note, however, that doesn't mean you can't invest in—and profit from—sustainability. Whether you're more swayed by resource scarcity or climate catastrophes, insurance premiums or stock prices, Simon Kuznets or Hurricane Sandy, it's hard to deny what's going on: the economic scales are tipping in favor of sustainability.

Indeed, businesses large and small are beginning to realize that, like a mob boss, Mother Nature calls in her debts unexpectedly, charges steep interest, and makes you take a beating—sometimes with gale force winds. As a result, many enterprises are doing something different, something new. They're consuming less of nature's bounty and conserving more of it. They're realizing that, as low as the environment can drive a company's P&L, sustainability can lift it even more. And they're discovering that Houshi's 1,300-year-old mantra is as relevant in the twenty-first century as it was in the eighth. Yes, Mother Nature may be a brutal creditor, but she also makes a generous business partner.

Sustainability is, you might say, an offer the private sector can't refuse.

5

CORPORATE CLIMATE CHANGE

"You better start swimming
or you'll sink like a stone,
for the times they are a-changin'."
—Bob Dylan

IT WAS A BEAUTIFUL DAY FOR FLYING, and as the plane
made its way up the Eastern Seaboard toward New England,
we passed over rural Pennsylvania. I took a break from edit-
ing the speech I was going to deliver the next day and gazed
down at the scenery below. The Alleghenies were awash in fall
colors, and the farmland in the valleys was still emerald green.
But what really caught my eye were the dozen or so aqua-blue
swimming pools dotting the landscape, next to what appeared
to be mountaintop getaways.

Man, I thought, *how great would it be to live in one of those!*

But before my retirement fantasy was able to play itself out any further, I peered a little closer. I realized these properties were anything but dream homes. They were so-called fracking operations, which drill into shale rock formations deep underground to extract oil and natural gas. Fracking fluids—water mixed with a concoction of chemicals—are blasted in, causing fissures in the rock, releasing the oil or gas, and forcing it to the surface. The "mountaintop getaways" I was coveting were actually fracking sites. The "swimming pools" I daydreamed about taking a dip in were water reservoirs used for hydraulic fracturing.

I turned back to my speech with a new sense of urgency. I was on my way to Hartford, Connecticut, to speak to the top executives of United Technologies Corporation (UTC). The topic of my talk: industry and sustainability.

UTC is one of the largest manufacturers in the world, and one of the world's largest corporations, period. It's the parent company of several famous American brands, including Carrier, Pratt & Whitney, and Otis Elevators. I know a lot about its businesses because I spent twenty-five years at Carrier before leaving the company in 2001 to start a consulting firm, after which, in 2004, I became the full-time CEO of USGBC.

When we touched down in Hartford, I started to get a little nervous. This would be my first time back to UTC headquarters since I had left eleven years earlier. As a former Carrier executive who went on to lead one of the world's largest sustainability organizations, I wasn't sure how I'd be received. In this corporate landscape I might have been a familiar face, but

I certainly wasn't a known commodity. I had spent the past several years as the only executive in rooms full of environmentalists; now I was about to be the only environmentalist in a room full of executives. I was used to giving talks in front of large audiences, at conferences and conventions, but many of those were in front of groups who shared my priorities. Speaking to the leadership of a Fortune 50 company would be a whole different ball game.

The auditorium was packed. I looked out at the audience of 400 people, and I could only imagine what they were thinking, looking back at me. Sure, I was *dressed* like a businessman in my suit and tie, but these folks knew my organization and my title. No doubt, they were sitting there waiting for me to shame them with examples of the private sector's environmental transgressions. But then I took the podium, looked down at my notes, and began to tell the executives of UTC that their company was helping save the planet.

If that's not what *you* expected, imagine how little *they* expected it. But it's the truth.

Between 2006 and 2014, UTC reduced its greenhouse gas emissions by 30 percent. It cut its company-wide water consumption by 33 percent. And it reduced total industrial process waste by 35 percent. These are astonishing numbers when you take a step back and consider the context. UTC builds jet engines, advanced aerospace systems, elevators, HVAC and refrigeration equipment, fire and security solutions, and even life support systems for the International Space Station!

We're talking about a manufacturing conglomerate that tallied $65.1 *billion* in net sales in 2014. For a company of this size, reducing waste isn't just recycling empty yogurt cups in the employee cafeteria. Reducing water consumption isn't just asking folks to "let it mellow when it's yellow." Reducing greenhouse gas emissions isn't just printing double-sided or turning computer monitors off at the end of the workday. No, to achieve the sustainability outcomes listed above, UTC has made *enormous* changes in its manufacturing operations (including, I'm proud to say, opening twelve LEED-certified factories around the world).

But here's the thing: The company's leaders didn't do all this to benefit the planet alone. *They did it to benefit their shareholders.* UTC is becoming more sustainable for a simple, powerful reason, one that has motivated every enterprise and entrepreneur throughout history: to make more money.

By reducing waste, emissions, and water usage, UTC has dramatically reduced costs. And while my friend Geraud Darnis, president and CEO of UTC Building & Industrial Systems, appreciates the aggregated savings from UTC's twelve LEED-certified factories, he appreciates the market upside even more. "The more that building developers, owners, and tenants embrace sustainability, the more we'll grow with those opportunities by providing solutions such as high-efficiency chillers, elevators that return energy to a building's electrical grid, and integrated systems," Darnis told me recently. "We also have a significant opportunity to reduce the environmental impact of food waste by extending food supplies with the cold chain—which includes marine container refrigeration, truck and trailer refrigeration, and food retail refrigeration—that will help feed a hungry and growing world."

The markets have rewarded UTC for its efforts. During the same eight-year period in which the company was increasing profitability by focusing on sustainability, its stock price climbed by a whopping 105 percent.

"Well," you might say, "that's just one company, albeit a big one. Who cares?"

I'll tell you who cares: Wall Street! Pension funds, mutual funds, and university endowments care, too, because UTC is not an outlier. It's part of a bigger transformation that's beginning to take shape in American and global business. UTC's sustainability practices put it well ahead of the curve, but by no means out of the mainstream. UTC is one of a growing number of companies pursuing real resource efficiency and waste reduction, achieving real cost savings as a result, and driving sales, profits, innovation, and growth—all at once.

These are the greenthinkers, and their names just might surprise you.

———

If you've ordered a Dell laptop since 2009, there's a good chance there was something different about it. I'm not talking about the processor or the amount of RAM or the quality of the screen. I'm not even talking about the computer. I mean the packaging it came in.

In a 2012 story for *Green Manufacturer,* Oliver Campbell, Dell's director of packaging procurement, described an initiative that took him and his team halfway around the world to China, on a quest for packaging materials that were better for their customers, better for the environment, and better for business. And they found just what they were looking for: bamboo.

Bamboo might be best known as a food for pandas, but it's also considered a rapid renewable resource because, well, it grows so rapidly—as much as two feet a day, which means it can be harvested earlier than other hardwoods. And while bamboo is relatively light, it is also unbelievably strong.

Of course, Dell wanted to make sure it didn't use just any bamboo—particularly not if it would affect the pandas. As Campbell told *Green Manufacturer,* "We've walked the supply chain in Jiangxi Province in China several times, inspecting their harvesting practices. The harvesting of the bamboo trees is done via selective cutting, not clear cutting, and bamboo naturally regenerates."

Switching to bamboo helped Dell lower its packaging and shipping costs and in the process, according to Campbell, contributed to savings of "more than $20 million just due to the use of greener packaging." It's a great story about a big company doing right by the environment. But here's the best part: In the past few years, as the cost of bamboo has risen with demand, Dell has transitioned to *other* forms of sustainable packaging, including wheat straw– and even mushroom-based packaging (more on this in chapter 8). Their experiment with bamboo opened their eyes to the benefits—ecological *and* monetary—of sustainable packaging. According to the company's 2015 Corporate Responsibility report, "As a result of our efforts, at the end of FY15, 100 percent of the packaging for Dell tablet shipments and 92 percent of the packaging for laptop shipments was recyclable or compostable—up from 86 percent and 85 percent, respectively, in FY14." Dell's continued focus on environmentally friendly packaging has resulted in "saving a cumulative $53.3 million in costs and avoiding 31.3 million pounds of packaging."

Dell has made its business better, greener, and more profitable by making a specific, strategic change in an existing production system. But in order to make internal changes such as these, companies need to understand where their excess environmental costs are coming from.

In 2011, German sportswear company Puma issued its first Environmental Profit and Loss (EP&L) report, which showed that the environmental impact of the company's operations and those of its suppliers in the prior year was equal to nearly €145 million. That's slightly more than 10 percent of Puma's 2010 profits! Of this massive cost, Puma learned that 94 percent—or €137 million—came from its supply chain, including 57 percent (or €83 million) from raw materials. Not long after, the company started making products—shoes, T-shirts, jackets, and backpacks—that are totally biodegradable or recyclable. Puma calls the line "InCycle" and has used the same EP&L concept to compare the impact of these products. In a 2013 report, PwC cited Puma as a sustainability case study, stating that "the environmental impact of its InCycle shoe is nearly a third less than its conventional suede shoe and equivalent to €2.95, or 3 percent of the retail price." According to Puma, in the process of making these InCycle shoes, the company also uses 21 percent less water and 20 percent less land, and produces 35 percent fewer greenhouse gas emissions and 60 percent less waste.

In an effort to further reduce costs and waste, the company has also begun to eliminate that trusty old friend of footwear: the shoebox. Working with renowned designer Yves Béhar, Puma has created what it calls the "Clever Little Bag," an alternative packaging for its shoes that has already saved the company 5,400 tons of cardboard. As Alan McGill of PwC put it, "Fundamentally, Puma's analysis is about risk management for the environment, and for business, because you cannot separate the two."

The Innovation Bottom Line, a joint report from the MIT Sloan Management Review and the Boston Consulting Group, confirms that this kind of internal examination and reflection is necessary for sustainable strategies to drive profits. According to Jason Jay, the director of the MIT Sloan Initiative for Sustainable Business and Society, "Companies can find ways to solve [their sustainability] problems and profit in the process. But to do so takes innovation in management practices, business models, and market infrastructures."

In other words, sustainability isn't about selling green gadgets like a solar-powered device that chases away garden moles. (No, I don't own one, but yes, I almost bought it.) Corporations like Dell and Puma are realizing that the truly sustainable innovations are not necessarily the ones that roll off the assembly line. Rather, the sustainable innovation is *the assembly line itself*—how products are made, how materials are sourced, and how energy is conserved.

The potential economic savings of a sustainable supply chain is mind-boggling—which is why, according to a 2011 survey by McKinsey & Company, "improving operational efficiency and lowering costs" now edges out "corporate reputation" as the number one reason corporate executives are addressing sustainability issues. And while 51 percent of companies responded by saying they were "managing corporate reputation for sustainability," 61 percent stated they were "reducing waste" and 63 percent said they were "reducing energy use."

Take Nestlé, for instance, which buys more coffee beans than any other corporation in the world. As you can imagine, coffee grounds are a major by-product of its manufacturing processes. The company used to send these grounds to landfills. But then management realized something: By burning the coffee grounds instead of disposing of them, they could produce steam, a source of power in many of their factories. According to *The Innovation Bottom Line*, "Some 60 percent of the steam the company uses now comes from burning coffee grounds, significantly reducing Nestlé's reliance on natural gas. In addition, in over twenty years, the company was able to divert 1.24 million tons of coffee grounds away from landfills."

The Ford Motor Company has also turned trash into treasure, most notably at its LEED-certified plant along the Rouge River in Michigan. In an interview with *McKinsey Quarterly*, Bill Ford, the company's chairman (and Henry's great-grandson), said that the plant was capturing the fumes from its paint shop and transforming them into energy. The company also uses plants—including a massive green roof—to break down "heavy metals and other junk," and then filter it into clean water that is piped back into the factory. As Bill Ford told McKinsey, "A lot of these things were big cost savers as well as the right thing to do for the environment." He continues, "For us, sustainability in its broadest sense is about economic sustainability. It's not just about sustainability for environmental reasons—if you don't have a sustainable business model, none of the rest matters."

Or, as one of the chief architects behind the Rouge River project, my friend and sustainability expert Bill McDonough, put it: "The math was simple and compelling: the living roof offered millions of dollars in savings, with the landscape thrown in for free. Kind of gets your attention."

Yes, it does.

The immediate economic benefits of sustainability are indeed grabbing the attention of many major corporations. For instance, Procter & Gamble reported in April 2013 that forty-five of its plants send no manufacturing waste to landfills.

Zero. Nada. Zilch. Instead, various P&G plants have devised new ways to conserve and transform at the same time, creating value in the process. According to the company, in Mexico, a Charmin toilet paper plant is transforming sludge into roof tiles for local homes. In the UK, Gillette is composting shaving cream waste. In the U.S., Pampers is turning the scraps from making baby wipes into upholstery stuffing. Clearly, each of these initiatives is great from a conservation perspective. But I guarantee you, that's not what the folks in P&G's C-suite care most about. I'm sure they're much more interested in the $1 billion in value that's been created by their commitment to sustainability.

Of course, P&G is not alone. Their major competitor, Unilever, announced its Sustainable Living Plan in 2010, in order to "double the size of our business while reducing our environmental footprint, and increasing our positive social impact." The SLP has indeed transformed the way Unilever does business. It's also proven just how lucrative sustainability can be. Over the past 5 years, Unilever has grown by an average of 4.9 percent per year, and its stock price has shot up by 40 percent. At the same time, Unilever has found new ways to cut costs by culling carbon emissions. In manufacturing alone, Unilever has reduced its emissions by 37 percent since 2008, and saved more than €400 million, thanks to its sustainability efforts.

Increasingly, companies are boosting their margins by squeezing the most out of every dollar and every input. They're making more by wasting less. This is, as we've seen, a good thing—good for the environment, good for the bottom line. All businesses want to cut costs and spend less. But the "missing link" that no one seems to focus on is that these companies are also *earning more*. Companies like Unilever and P&G that pursue sustainability initiatives are seeing their efforts pay off on both ends of the balance sheet. The bottom line is improved as they make supply chains more efficient (not to mention the new product innovation driven by seeing the world through a sustainable lens). As for the top line, their revenues are climbing as respect for their brands and demand for their products rises as well. In other words, sustainability doesn't just help corporations get a bigger piece of the pie—it helps them *grow* the pie, too.

As early as 2007, an industry study from investment banking firm Goldman Sachs recognized this. The report stated, "More capital is now focused on sustainable business models, and the market is rewarding leaders and new entrants in a way that could scarcely have been predicted even fifteen years ago." Why? One reason is because consumer patterns, in particular, have evolved.

In 1992—fifteen years before that Goldman Sachs report —companies didn't do much to advertise their sustainability efforts or the sustainable aspects of their products. The *ENERGY STAR* label had just been introduced and was being stamped only on computers and monitors. There weren't many customers who even knew what "sustainability" meant, let alone cared enough about it to change their patterns of consumption. At that time a "green shopper" was thought to be a tie-dye enthusiast who would have considered Whole Foods "too commercial." In order to buy his organic kale, he would slap on his Birkenstocks, hop on his bicycle, and pedal his way to the nearest farmers' market.

But Mr. Birkenstocks is not the typical green consumer anymore, if he ever was. Today, the data shows that the most accurate phrase to describe green shoppers is "most of us." The majority of consumers are now rewarding companies for going green and punishing those whose business practices harm the environment or human health. According to the global consulting firm Deloitte, 54 percent of consumers "consider sustainability to be one of their decision-making factors in product and store selection." Even more impressive is the fact that green shoppers aren't just buying green; they're *spending* it, too. According to Deloitte, "Contrary to the popular myth that the green shopper is an austere idealist, *they actually buy more and shop more often* than the typical shopper . . . All the data suggests that this is a very desirable target shopper."

These green shoppers have tremendous potential to drive change and reshape the market through one of the most powerful economic forces: their demand. The greater the desire for sustainable products, the larger the supply will become over time. That means each of us has innumerable, daily opportunities to build a more sustainable world through our individual purchasing power. Corporations like Walmart, Target, Kroger, Home Depot, Amazon, and countless others are watching these purchases. They're tracking what you buy, when, how much, and where. And if consumers want sustainable products, that's what Corporate America will produce. In the age of big data, no purchase goes unnoticed. Sure, what you buy is just a blip on the radar, but large companies are paying attention to those blips. And the smartest ones are changing their business models as a result.

Can you guess what Adidas, BMW, Intel, Samsung, General Mills, Siemens, and General Electric have in common? They are all on the Corporate Knights 2015 list of the world's one hundred most sustainable companies, and it's hard to ignore the impact that sustainability is having on these companies' top lines. Siemens reports that in 2014 its Environmental Portfolio brought in €33 billion for the company (and also eliminated 428 million tons of CO_2 emissions for its customers). Since its inception in 2005, GE's Ecomagination program has added $200 billion to the company's top line, and sales from its green products have grown four times as fast as the company's other industrial product lines.

For Natura, a Brazilian cosmetics company founded in the late 1960s, sustainability isn't just their strategy; it's their brand. The company's name, Natura, obviously means "nature." And the company's slogan—"*Bem estar bem*"—translates as "Well-being/being well." In Portuguese, it carries roughly the same meaning as the common English maxim that those of us in the green building industry say over and over: "We can do well by doing good." And make no mistake: Natura has done very well for its shareholders by doing good for the environment.

Over the years, Natura has consulted with everyone from nongovernmental organizations to rural Amazon communities to find better natural ingredients for its products—and newer, more sustainable ways to extract them. According to the *Guardian*, the company uses data it gets from suppliers—including figures for emissions, water usage, and waste—to calculate the environmental cost of a particular source. Natura then "uses a 'shadow price' for these factors to select suppliers with the lightest footprint, which will also create financial benefits." This sustainable sourcing not only has helped save money and the rain forest but, according to chief executive Alessandro Carlucci, has had a "big influence" on customers across Latin America, and even as far away as France, who are increasingly choosing sustainably sourced products.

Natura's strategy has paid off big-time. From 2011 to 2014, Natura experienced four straight years of revenue growth and increasing profits. And in 2014, brand consultancy Interbrand named Natura the number one retail brand in Latin America.

Bem estar bem. Doing well by doing good isn't just a nice sentiment any more. It's a proven business strategy.

———

In 1885, America was in the middle of the second Industrial Revolution. Electric lights were beginning to illuminate streets and homes. The first skyscraper—all ten floors of it—had just been built in Chicago. And in Wisconsin, a man named Warren Johnson was starting a business.

Two years before, in 1883, Johnson had secured a patent for the first electric thermostat. He came to Milwaukee to turn that invention into an enterprise, providing "domestic harmony and budget savings" to buildings large and small. He called his business the Johnson Electric Service Company, and in 1974 the company was rebranded Johnson Controls, Inc. Perhaps the name rings a bell. Over the past century, Johnson Controls has become one of the foremost global players in climate control and energy efficiency. In fact, according to the Fortune 500 in 2015, Johnson Controls was the sixty-sixth-largest company in America—ten spots ahead of Goldman Sachs—posting almost $44 billion in revenue.

As you probably guessed, the company doesn't just make thermostats anymore. Johnson Controls is a huge corporation, and it takes on equally huge projects—including the retrofitting of one of America's biggest and most famous office buildings: the Empire State Building, which first opened its doors in 1931. Like many buildings of its era, for a long time it bled money due to ineffective or nonexistent insulation and inefficient heating and cooling systems. Until recently, the costs of heating and cooling the building were astronomical. As Clay Nesler, the vice president for global energy and sustainability for Johnson Controls, jokingly told me, "The building did a pretty good job helping to heat outdoor Manhattan."

As part of the massive retrofit, Johnson Controls—working with Empire State Building ownership and partners Jones Lasalle, the Rocky Mountain Institute, and the C40/Clinton Climate Initiative—added insulation behind the radiators, upgraded the motors and added variable speed drives to dated chillers, installed high-efficiency lighting, and put in wireless building control systems. But its most impressive feat was that every night, under the cover of darkness, dozens of windows were quietly removed. Unbeknownst to thousands of office workers and tourists who enter the Empire State Building each day, there was a window-processing center on its fifth floor. There, each window was filled with an inert gas and remanufactured with a special, suspended solar control film that blocks light and better regulates temperature—transforming the old double-paned windows into more efficient triple-paned windows without the need for any more glass. On the north side of the building, these new and improved windows were remanufactured to let in more light; on the other three sides, they were rebuilt to block heat. An elite team from a company called Serious Energy worked tirelessly until all 6,514 windows were replaced. "Most people came in the next day and thought we had just cleaned the windows," Clay said. "But actually, we had tripled the efficiency."

While the tourists and the tenants may not have seen the difference, the building owners did. From 2011 to 2013, the retrofit project had already racked up about $7.5 million in energy savings. The Empire State Building used to be the tallest building in the country, but now it has a new distinction: the tallest *energy-efficient* building in the country.

When people marvel at New York City's awesome skyline, they don't look at the Empire State Building and think *green*. They look at the Empire State Building and think *great*. The same goes for our economy. Just like the Empire State Building, our economy has the structure to stay great for years to come. We don't need to tear it down; we just need to retrofit it.

Retrofitting takes time. It happens piece by piece, window by window, building by building, company by company. We can't expect to wake up one day and find ourselves living in a brave, new, sustainable world. That kind of "green wishing" is just as bad as greenwashing. But if the list of companies in this chapter is any indication, our world is already headed in a direction that is as green as it is great.

6

SUSTAINABLE
DEVELOPMENT

*"Saving the planet is better economics
than burning it up."*
—*Bill Clinton*

IMAGINE THAT YOU'RE THE LEADER of a very large, very poor nation. The vast majority of your people live in extreme poverty. A third of your rural population is illiterate. Only half of all children go to high school. Life expectancy for your citizens is well below that of developed nations.

As the head of this failing state, what would you do to turn things around? Actually, a better question might be: What *wouldn't* you do?

This isn't a hypothetical scenario. This was the reality facing China's leadership before the country implemented economic reforms that paved the way for three decades of unprecedented development. According to the World Bank, Chinese economic growth "has lifted more than 500 million people out of poverty." Life expectancy is nearly thirty-two years higher than it was in 1960. The child mortality rate has plummeted. The adult literacy rate is 95 percent, and 92 percent of children are enrolled in secondary school. China has a thriving middle class and is now, by some measures, the world's largest economy.

The improved material well-being of the Chinese people has been nothing short of a miracle. The environmental impact of this economic development, however, has been nothing short of a catastrophe.

It doesn't take a PhD to see the correlation between the growth of China's economy and the widespread devastation of its environment. One ugly image of this devastation was on horrific display in the Huangpu River in March 2013, when 16,000 rotting and diseased pig carcasses were discovered in the water. It was an ecological abomination by any measure, and especially disturbing when you consider that the Huangpu supplies drinking water to residents of Shanghai. But pig carcasses, unfortunately, are simply the most visible—and not necessarily the most harmful—contaminant found in China's rivers, streams, and aquifers, which are full of toxic industrial chemicals, pesticides, fertilizers, and raw sewage. As the *Guardian* reported in 2014, "Nearly 60 percent of China's underground water is polluted."

And then there is China's air pollution. The air quality index (AQI) is based on U.S. Environmental Protection Agency standards. As *The Economist* has reported, "Any reading above 100 is deemed 'unhealthy for sensitive groups,' and . . . anything above 400 is rated 'hazardous' for all." Air quality in China, however, regularly exceeds that rating by a staggering margin. On January 12, 2013, for example, Beijing registered an AQI of 755. But you don't need a fancy test to know the air quality in China is horrible. I've been to China nearly twice a year for the past six years. The air literally chokes you.

This pollution is taking a brutal toll on the Chinese people. The 2010 Global Burden of Disease Study found that China's air pollution led to 1.2 million premature deaths that year. And a 2013 study in the *Proceedings of the National Academies of Sciences* estimated that coal pollution has reduced life expectancy by 5.5 years for almost 500 *million* people living in northern China. In recent years, there have been numerous stories of "cancer villages," where residents—often living close to heavy industry or relying on tainted water—have sky-high rates of the disease.

All of this is beyond tragic, and all too familiar to me.

My dad worked for much of his adult life in a print shop. Every Saturday morning, he'd take me along to check on a couple of his jobs. Above all, I remember the smell—a strong, oppressive scent. In fact, to call it a "scent" doesn't even capture it. It was a total body experience, and not a pleasant one. You'd walk inside, and within about three minutes you'd feel as if you were high on the vapors of glue, paint thinner, and a chemist's trove of toxins. My lips swelled. My skin itched.

This was where my dad worked for more than twenty years. He died of a brain tumor when he was fifty-four years old.

Tragically, we didn't know as much in those days about the effects of chemicals and contaminants on human health. There was no government council, no union committee that went to my dad's employer and said, "Hey, you can't let your people work in those rooms without proper ventilation, without proper testing, without proper safeguards." We just didn't know enough.

Having lost my dad to the effects of environmental pollution, I know the heartache endured millions of times over in China today. I wish no one ever had to suffer the loss of a loved one because they were exposed to dangerous toxins on the job or in their community. Breathing clean air, drinking clean water, living and working in safety and relative comfort—these things aren't first-world luxuries. They are basic human rights.

But they're not the *only* basic human rights. There's also the right to have a place to live, food to eat, a job to support your family, a school where your kids can get a decent education, and access to health care. And that's where the debate on the morality and acceptability of China's economic growth gets a lot more complicated.

Think back to the hypothetical at the beginning of this chapter. If you were the leader of a country so impoverished that people were starving to death, is there anything you wouldn't do to grow the economy and lift your nation out of poverty? I've thought about this question, and it didn't take me long to come up with an answer. No, there is nothing I wouldn't do. I'd do *anything*.

That's exactly what China's leaders decided in the late 1970s. They recognized that rapid economic growth was their people's only chance to escape abject poverty. And the only way to achieve that growth was to turn China into a manufacturing powerhouse that sold goods all around the world. Doing so required the mining and utilization of massive quantities of oil, coal, heavy metals, chemicals, and other raw materials. Extracting these resources in such abundance is terrible for the Earth and just as bad for human health. But this was the *only way out* for a country and a people that didn't have the education, the technology, or the infrastructure to propel their economy using other means.

I care deeply about our planet and preserving it for future generations, but the planet doesn't much matter if the people who live on it are suffering, starving, and dying. And that's why, even though I hate the environmental havoc that has occurred in China as a result of its average 10 percent growth in GDP for thirty consecutive years, I don't blame its leadership. And I don't envy the choice they had to make—ensuring the well-being of a billion people, at the expense of the health of millions of people and their natural ecosystems. It's not quite Sophie's choice, but it isn't far off.

Let's not forget that America essentially followed the same trajectory during our own period of industrialization. The only difference is, we didn't know that plundering the Earth was so damaging to human health, nor did we realize how much irreparable harm we were doing to our environment, and how delicate our environment really was—and is. Then again, even if we'd had that knowledge, I doubt it would have stopped us from building coal plants and cutting down old-growth forests. Immediate economic interests would have—and always will—come first. That's just the way it is.

Of course, China's industrialization is happening faster and on a far bigger scale than what we experienced in America, or anything we've seen anywhere in the world—ever. The immensity of China's growth stretches the imagination, but so does the distance that country has yet to travel. According to the *Wall Street Journal,* some 82 million people in China still live on less than one dollar a day. Meanwhile, the population continues to grow; it's projected to hit 1.4 billion by 2026.

Continued rapid economic growth is essential to improving the lives of the Chinese people. But this growth—if it looks anything like that of the past thirty years—will further devastate China's environment, which has already deteriorated to the point that pollution is killing more than a million of its citizens each year and reducing the life expectancy of hundreds of millions.

We're at a familiar crossroads, it would seem. China must choose: profit or planet. It can't have both, right?

Wrong.

Environmental degradation is beginning to cost the Chinese

people more than just their health and quality of life. It's hitting the Chinese *economy* hard, too.

For starters, it's making it tougher for Chinese companies to attract talent. About one-third of China's registered expat population lives in Beijing, and many are wondering if working in China is worth the threat to their health and that of their families. As one prominent Beijing doctor told the *Financial Times*, "Recruitment is getting harder for all companies—how do you convince people to come work in the most polluted city in the world?" Huang Xiaoping, who runs a Chinese recruitment firm, told the *Christian Science Monitor* that the country's pollution problem "will be a big challenge," adding, "environmental problems could become a big obstacle to future economic growth."

These fears are more than justified; they've also been quantified. According to the *New York Times*, the Chinese government's own Academy of Environmental Planning has estimated that the negative effect of pollution on China's economy has tripled—at least—since 2004. As the *Times* reported, "The cost of environmental degradation in China was about $230 billion in 2010, or 3.5 percent of the nation's gross domestic product."

That might not sound like a lot, but consider that for the American economy, in any given year, 3.5 percent is the difference between strong growth and a recession. And these estimates are notoriously conservative. The *Times* noted that "the $230 billion figure is incomplete because the researchers did not have a full set of data." According to a 2013 report from the World Bank and China's Development Resource Center of the State Council, "The costs of environmental degradation and resource depletion in China are estimated to approach 10 percent of GDP, of which air pollution accounts for 6.5 percent, water pollution 2.1 percent, and soil degradation 1.1 percent." If a 3.5 percent hit is the difference between strong growth and recession, you can imagine that a 10 percent hit would be Greatly Depressing.

Governments, like people, respond to incentives. The Chinese leadership knows that to maintain its firm grip on power, it has to keep the Chinese people happy. For a long time, that meant growing the economy regardless of the environmental cost and the collateral damage to the health of some Chinese citizens. But now, the politburo is sensing a structural shift in its incentives. To retain power, it has to protect the environment *while* growing the economy. Environmentalism and economic growth in China are becoming intertwined—a fact that has tremendous, global implications.

In 2012, Chen Jiping, a former leader of the Chinese Communist Party's Committee of Political and Legislative Affairs, noted that pollution was the main cause of political protest in China. Type "Chinese environmental protest" into Google and you'll find scores of pictures of Chinese citizens packing the streets, wearing surgical masks, and waving signs decrying the environmental costs of rapid industrialization. In June 2015, *Forbes* reported, "Mass environmental protests continue to gain strength in China. Within the last couple of months thousands of people in different parts of the country have vocally, and in some cases violently, railed against polluting chemical plants, waste incinerator projects, and coal-fired power plant expansions."

Anyone who remembers what happened in Tiananmen Square in 1989 knows how the Chinese government feels about social unrest. So, as you can imagine, all this citizen upheaval about the environment has captured the attention of leaders in Beijing. In March 2013, premier Wen Jiabao gave a speech unveiling the country's annual budget, in which he acknowledged the pace of Chinese growth as "unbalanced, uncoordinated, and unsustainable." According to the *Guardian*, Jiabao "stressed green issues—the budget promises an 18.8 percent boost for energy conservation and environmental protection, to 210bn yuan." That's about $34 billion—nothing to sneeze at.

Meanwhile, China's twelfth Five-Year Plan for 2011 to 2015 (the economic planning documents released by the governing Communist Party every half decade) has focused intently on growing seven "strategic emerging industries," including new energy, environmental protection, and alternative energy automotive, to 8 percent of GDP in 2015, and to 15 percent of GDP in 2020. The Climate Group's analysis of the plan concluded, "China's low-carbon ambitions are accelerating and will bend the nation's carbon emissions growth curve in the next five years." Not just slow it or smooth it, but *bend* it.

In 2013, the Chinese government also announced the details of a carbon-trading program, which they introduced in seven cities and provinces that year. Yes, you read that correctly. While we environmentalists in America can only dream of the day when Congress implements a U.S. cap-and-trade system, China's is already up and running. China has also spent a hefty sum on solar and wind in recent years. In 2014, China invested more than $80 billion in renewable energy—more than Europe and the United States *combined*.

Speaking of America, you may have heard about the major climate announcement President Barack Obama and President Xi Jinping made in November 2014. For their part, Chinese government leaders declared they would "peak CO_2 emissions around 2030, with the intention to try to peak early, and to increase the non–fossil fuel share of all energy to around 20 percent by 2030." This was a tremendous moment—the world's two biggest polluters finally cooperating on climate and clean energy. Not only that, it was also historic; according to the White House, this "marks the first time China has agreed to peak its CO_2 emissions."

Now, I'll be honest. I don't trust China—or any country, for that matter—to do what's right for the environment. But I *do* trust China's government to do what's right for its economy and for its self-preservation. Chinese leadership isn't taking these monumental steps to become a better environmental steward because it's the moral thing to do, or for the publicity. They're doing it because, from both an economic and a political perspective, environmental sustainability is now an imperative. In other words, what we're seeing in China is that environmental degradation is no longer just a consequence of economic growth—*it's a threat to growth itself.*

In years to come, China will take further steps—and likely even more significant and increasingly radical steps—to safeguard the health of both its environment and its people. Again, not because China's leaders have had a tree-hugging conversion, but because it's the only viable, long-term strategy for China's continued economic development as a nation.

Let me come right out and say it: This is unprecedented. It's exciting. And it's just the beginning.

China is just one country—even if it's one of the most important in terms of its environmental and economic impact. What about the rest of the world? It turns out that the same dynamic at work in China is emerging elsewhere. Global environmental devastation is upending the macroeconomic fundamentals not only in China, but also throughout the developing world. It's easy to see why. Just like in China, pollution now has a measurable impact on the economies of developing nations.

In India, for example, 80 percent of the country's sewage flows right into its rivers, including its main sources of drinking water. Air pollution in India is 6 times worse than it was in 2000, and kills an estimated 620,000 people each year. Researchers at the World Bank estimate that environmental damage cost India about $80 billion in 2009, the equivalent of *5.7 percent* of its GDP.

As you might imagine, the situation is just as dire elsewhere. Throughout the 2000s, the World Bank published a series of Country Environmental Analyses (CEAs), each of which looked to quantify the effect of environmental devastation on an individual country's economy. And while the data comes from all around the world, and came out across multiple years, the results are shockingly—horrifyingly—similar.

A 2006 report states, "In Colombia, lack of access to clean water, poor or nonexistent sanitation services, and indoor air pollution are among the principal causes of illness and death, predominantly for children and women in poor households. The effects of these principal causes of environmental degradation are estimated to cost more than 3.7 percent of Colombia's GDP."

Meanwhile, that same year, Pakistan's CEA reported, "Conservative estimates presented in this report suggest that environmental degradation costs the country at least 6 percent of GDP."

The following year, the CEA for Ghana stated, "Recent estimates of the cost of natural resource and environmental degradation suggest that the equivalent of 9.6 percent of GDP is lost annually through unsustainable management of the country's forests and land resources and through health costs related to water supply and sanitation, and indoor and outdoor air pollution."

The 2008 Nepal CEA reads: "These environmental risk factors have resulted in premature death and disease, especially among the poor and vulnerable groups, and are placing increased health costs and a significant economic burden on the country, estimated at close to US$258 million or nearly 3.5 percent of the country's GDP."

I could keep going, but you get the idea. Pollution is directly impacting prosperity in parts of the world where prosperity is desperately needed. And the scale of that impact is terrifying. There are nearly 200 countries in the world. Imagine adding up the *global* cost of pollution and environmental devastation—an analysis that, to my surprise, no one has yet performed. We can easily guess the outcome. The tally would be *trillions* of dollars—dollars that are literally going up in smoke.

It's clear that the old model of economic growth is no longer viable. In fact, in aggregate, the old model is a measurable drag on growth that essentially amounts to a *global environmental depression.*

But imagine for a moment that these costs don't exist. Imagine that we've eliminated millions of unnecessary, premature deaths. Imagine that black smoke and yellow smog become clear blue sky, that industrial chemicals are cleansed from the water, that a century of carbon emissions are sucked out of the air. Imagine a world in which bull markets can throw off the yoke of pollution and run even faster. Imagine that people around the world can breathe clean air and drink clean water, not just some days, but *every* day. Imagine how these people—no longer being poisoned and sometimes killed by pollution—will need goods and services and jobs, and businesses to provide all three. Never mind the environmental transformation. Think about the *human* transformation. Think about the *economic* transformation: trillions of dollars of economic stimulus, *just by eliminating pollution.*

A world without pollution is a world in which opportunity is our most abundant natural resource—a world in which everything is going full speed because the light is always green. A decade ago, this might have been a fantasy, a pipe dream. But not anymore. The world is changing. And while a pollution-free future is a *long* way off, a significantly cleaner, healthier, and more profitable future is not.

Developing countries have every right to grow, to prosper, and to meet the urgent needs of their citizens. Pollution has been the by-product of this growth—an acceptable by-product, you might argue, considering that growth wouldn't have existed without it. Today, however, the equation is shifting. Pollution is increasingly a *barrier* to growth in the developing world. Sure enough, political leaders in developing countries are slowly awakening to the fact that profit and the planet are no longer mutually exclusive—that they're symbiotic, part of the same ecosystem.

Of course, not every government in the developing world is

taking bold actions like China. In fact, few of them are. China is awakening to this new paradigm first, perhaps because of the severity of the environmental devastation there, in addition to the fact that its political survival depends on it. China also has a central government that can make big changes practically overnight. But other governments are starting to address the environmental depressions that are dragging down their economies and their people. In 2012, India's Bureau of Energy Efficiency began implementing the Perform, Achieve, and Trade (PAT) Scheme, a market-based program designed to help reduce carbon emissions. In March 2013, Peru announced "an environmental state of emergency" in part of the Amazon rain forest, and the country's Ministry of the Environment established soil quality standards to protect the environment. The Brazilian government now requires all companies whose activities impact the environment to register with a government agency that monitors those activities.

These efforts are just the beginning. In the coming years, I know we'll see more and more developing nations change the way they do business. How can I be so sure? *Because they don't have a choice.*

But governments are only part of the equation. As I discussed in chapter 5, there is a growing army of greenthinking companies large and small, poised to deliver the innovations these governments will need going forward: smarter, cleaner, more sustainable, and more profitable ways to fuel, build, feed, and organize their economies. As governments in the developing world set targets or create incentives for sustainable economic growth, thousands of ambitious entrepreneurs and companies will step up to offer solutions.

We're already seeing this in India. Consider, for example, Asian Paints, the largest Indian paint company, based in Mumbai. As *Forbes* reported, after government regulations restricted the ways in which businesses could dispose of their liquid waste, Asian Paints resolved to stop producing liquid waste—completely. The chief strategy officer at Asian Paints expressed his relief that these innovations have lifted an "economic burden" off their shoulders. Not an environmental burden or a regulatory burden, but an *economic* one.

Members of the business community in India see not just environmental imperatives, but also economic opportunities. *Forbes* also reported in 2012 how a new company stepped in to turn pollution into a sustainable and profitable power source:

> The state of Bihar is India's poorest, with 85 percent of the people living off the power grid. Its chief crop is rice, which results in another burden: 1.8 billion kilograms of rice husks go to the landfill each year, where they produce methane, a gas that warms the globe. This is the business opportunity of Husk Power Systems, which is developing gasifiers to convert rice husks into electricity. Fifty kilograms of husks per hour can provide a modest amount of power to 500 people.

BioLite is another company seeking to turn an enormous environmental and human health disaster into an incredible economic opportunity. The World Health Organization (WHO) estimates that nearly 3 billion people cook on open fires, and 1.2 billion have no access to electricity. As a result, according to WHO, "Over four million people die prematurely from illness attributable to the household air pollution from cooking with solid fuels." These fires also emit a significant amount of greenhouse gases.

Rather than leave people with the impossible choice between eating and breathing, BioLite makes a stove that uses 50 percent less wood than a typical open fire and emits 94 percent less smoke and 91 percent less carbon monoxide. On top of that, the stove can convert thermal energy into electricity to power lights and charge cell phones. BioLite has established pilot programs for this stove in India, Ghana, and Uganda, and it sells smaller versions to campers in the United States to help underwrite their efforts in emerging markets.

BioLite makes its motives very clear on its website: "We believe in market-based approaches to poverty alleviation . . . This is not charity or a one-for-one model." The company may call its method a "market-based" solution, but I imagine that environmentalists may refer to it in the future simply as "a solution."

This is just a preview of what's on the horizon. In the coming years, economic necessity will demand an unwavering commitment in developing countries to sustainability from both the public and private sector.

―――――――

Today, we're on a disastrous path. But the good news is that government and business leaders around the world are starting to wake up to reality. The result is, we finally have a chance to break free from the tired global argument about who needs to do what to save our planet.

On one side, developing countries balk at the idea of emissions caps or other environmental compacts that would limit their economic growth. They note, rightly, that rich nations like America spent the past century growing their economies with the help of dirty fossil fuels and without being hampered by environmental regulations. Developed countries, meanwhile, countercharge that China and other rapidly industrializing nations want to spend the next century doing the same thing, despite the tremendous and irreversible consequences that will have for everyone on the planet.

This argument has been going on forever, and there's a good reason for that: It's an argument without a resolution. Everyone is right, and everyone is wrong. The simple fact is that *all* countries—developed and developing alike—use lots of dirty fossil fuels and do terrible things to the environment. Until very recently, it's been the only way to improve living standards and achieve economic growth.

Yes, a century's reliance on fossil fuels has put our planet in the perilous position it is today. But it has also made the lives of *billions* of human beings immeasurably better. People are living longer and healthier lives thanks to scientific and technological innovations that simply would not have been possible without large quantities of low-cost energy. An abundance of cheap oil, coal, and gas, combined with the desire for someone, somewhere to make a profit, is what has enabled countries around the globe to build modern societies.

For a long time, most people understood and accepted the trade-off that some level of environmental decay was the cost of a growing economy that raises standards of living. Cut down a few forests, pollute a few rivers, drive some species to the brink of extinction, and in return you can build a bunch of stuff to sell for a profit and create jobs and growth along the way. You could ignore the negatives—especially when you never saw them with your own eyes. But this old trade-off has become a rip-off, because today, environmental degradation is threatening people's lives and livelihoods.

Thankfully, for the first time in modern history, economic and environmental interests have begun to align. Environmentalists have long argued that you can't have a healthy economy without a healthy environment. They're right. But the argument never hit home before now, because environmental degradation wasn't impacting companies' bottom lines and countries' GDP. Now it is, in a big way.

It's also going to start shaping the future.

A couple of years ago, I read an article in the *New York Times* about parents in Beijing forbidding their kids from playing outside because of the city's terrible air pollution. It brought back memories of my own childhood in upstate New York, where the soot from the local factories interrupted my afterschool playtime. I would get out of school at 2:30 and have to run straight home to help get the laundry in, because at 3:05 the factories nearby would belch black soot over everything in the area.

So I know how those kids in Beijing feel. They want to run around, get into trouble with their friends, play, explore, and have fun. In other words, they want to be kids! But they can't. And they know why: the air is their enemy. Even if they can't put it into words, even if it hasn't yet risen to the level of a conscious thought, I know there is a powerful feeling bubbling up inside them, a feeling that will stay with them forever. They hate pollution—just like I did.

Hundreds of millions of kids are growing up right now, in China and around the world, in megacities and rural villages that are being devastated by an intolerable level of pollution and environmental chaos. Many of these kids have friends or relatives who will get sick from bad air, bad water, or the chemicals they don't even know they're being exposed to. Some of them will get sick themselves. Some will die.

This generation is growing up with the pollution that my generation created. It's a terrible thought. But they're also inheriting a world in which profit and the planet are, for the first time, inseparable. It's a difficult concept for folks my age to grasp. But the next generation will understand this intuitively. They'll profit at the *expense* of pollution—and that will be a beautiful thing.

7

THE FIVE R's

*"The source and fountain-head of genuine reform . . .
is an enlightened public opinion."*
—*Upton Sinclair*

IT'S THE UBIQUITOUS CATCHPHRASE of environmentalism,
an alliterative axiom known across the planet as the best hope
for trying to save it. We teach it to our kids in school. We
see it advertised on television, in grocery stores, on the street.
Jack Johnson even wrote a song about it. I'm talking about the
three-pillared temple of conservationism:

Reduce, reuse, recycle.

Today, the Three R's represent a conventional wisdom
deeply embedded in the public consciousness. It's not just that
we've memorized the motto; we've internalized the message.
In many ways, the decades-long effort to encourage individual
conservation has been an astounding success. In 2010, Gallup
polling showed that 85 percent of Americans reported taking

actions to reduce their energy consumption, and 90 percent said they had recycled in the past year. In fact, in 2013, Americans recycled and composted more than 87 million tons of their trash, which makes for a 34.3 percent recycling rate—more than twice the 1990 rate (16 percent), and five times the 1970 rate (6.6 percent). *Reduce, reuse, recycle* is easily the most effective marketing campaign in the history of the environmentalism. You could even say it's one of the best and most enduring campaigns in the history of advertising.

Unfortunately, the environmental movement has been a victim of its own success, because the Three R's will never save the planet.

Have you ever wondered what the environmental impact would be if *every* person in America recycled *everything* that was recyclable? Sure, recycling has caught on, but even if most of us do it, we're not recycling *all* the plastic, glass, paper, and metal we use every day. In fact, we recycle only a fraction of the products we consume—and it's not entirely our fault. The kind of pervasive recycling infrastructure we'd need to recycle everything we possibly could simply doesn't exist. Most communities have recycling programs, but not all do, and some are more robust than others.

That's why, in 2013 (as I pointed out above), Americans recycled only about a third of the municipal solid waste we produced. It's a significant percentage, no doubt—but the majority of our trash still goes to the landfill. According to the U.S. Environmental Protection Agency, the garbage we diverted in 2013 saved the equivalent of 186 million metric tons of greenhouse gases from being released into the atmosphere. Again, that's fantastic—but it amounted to only 2.8 percent of our nation's nearly 6.7 billion metric tons of greenhouse gas emissions that year.

Still, suspend disbelief for a moment and consider an America in which all 320 million of us put into the recycling bin every last Coke can, Starbucks cup, shampoo bottle, takeout container, pizza box, coat hanger from the drycleaners, and crumpled piece of tinfoil used to wrap up leftovers. Daydream with me about a nation that recycles reflexively, constantly, and ubiquitously. If we were somehow able to recycle not just one third but 100 percent of our refuse, the impact would be about 8 percent of our national carbon footprint. That would be an amazing feat—reducing our footprint by 8 percent through recycling alone! But what about the other 92 percent? We've been told that recycling is a third of the solution, along with reducing and reusing—but it solves less than a tenth of the problem.

Well then, what about reducing and reusing? Could we save the planet by conserving as much as possible and consuming as little as possible?

In 2007, a class at the Massachusetts Institute of Technology studied this question by examining the lifestyles of a wide swath of Americans to see how our individual carbon footprints varied. They estimated the average American's carbon footprint at about 20 tons of CO_2 equivalent per year—five times the world average. The MIT study aimed to determine how much Americans could reduce their individual impact by voluntarily—even radically—changing their lifestyles. What they found is stunning and totally counterintuitive. A homeless American has an environmental impact greater than the average person anywhere else on the planet. The same is true for a Buddhist monk in America and even a five-year-old child.

How can people who consume practically nothing have such massive carbon footprints? Well, the MIT study determined that there is a *floor*—a lower limit on our individual carbon emissions—that Americans cannot possibly, voluntarily get below. And I have bad news for you: it's not zero. Incredibly, it's 8.5 tons of CO_2 equivalent per year—more than twice the global average.

In the United States, the largest drivers of environmental degradation aren't individuals—they're institutions. For example, the MIT study made allotments for the public services we all use—roads, schools, hospitals, the military, you name it—in order to account for each American's individual carbon footprint. The study shows how these fundamental aspects of American life, aspects over which individuals have no control, increase our personal share of the nation's CO_2 emissions. Which is why the MIT study concluded that there are "very significant limits to voluntary actions to reduce impacts, both at a personal level and at a national level."

Now, some environmentalists would argue that if we all went off the grid—if the entire nation voluntarily gave up the conveniences of modern American life that result in our out-sized environmental impact—our problem would be solved. But that's no solution; it's insanity! It violates what I call "the cold beer litmus test": a solution that requires people to give up basic creature comforts just isn't viable.

Conservation will have a planet-saving result only when implemented not by great numbers of individuals, but by a great number of institutions—meaning the corporations and governments that are responsible for the goods and services we consume and utilize each and every day. Suggesting otherwise is nothing short of environmental malpractice. Which is not to say that the Three R's aren't important; they're critical. What I'm saying is that the Three R's alone—however radically implemented by individuals—won't get us there.

The problem isn't just that individual conservation efforts, even when combined, fail to have a large enough impact. The widespread acceptance of the Three R's has also resulted in a dangerous belief that *how much* we consume as a society is more important than *what* we consume. But as I've argued throughout this book, sustainability is about more than just conservation and carbon. It's about how the things we build and buy impact—or, more to the point, threaten—people's lives.

Sustainability is still a relatively new concept. The UN first defined sustainable development in 1987 as meeting "the needs of the present without compromising the ability of future generations to meet their own needs." According to the legislation that created the U.S. Environmental Protection

Agency (EPA), sustainability means working "to create and maintain the conditions under which humans and nature can exist in productive harmony, that permit fulfilling the social, economic, and other requirements of present and future generations." I don't disagree with either of those definitions, but I don't think it has to be nearly that complicated. To me, sustainability is simply about helping people live longer and healthier lives—both now and in the future. If we are ever going to realize the sustainable world we badly want and desperately need, we have to update the Three R's to reflect this fundamental truth.

Fortunately, there are two more R's that have the potential to drive meaningful change on a massive scale: *report* and *review*. By encouraging (or requiring) the private sector to report the contents of the products we consume, and by reviewing those contents to determine their human health and environmental impacts, we can instigate the kind of market and social transformation that has thus far eluded us. Indeed, history shows that transparency—the mere act of reporting and reviewing—can dramatically change the behavior of consumers, governments, and corporations alike.

————

If you know me, you know that I love food. I love the smell of home cooking, I love dining out at new restaurants, and I love discovering amazing dishes when I travel. You might even call me a "foodie." Of course, I'm always proud when any restaurant earns a LEED certification. But when I think about the relationship between sustainability and transparency, instead of energy-efficient buildings I often think about food—not because it makes me hungry, but because there is perhaps no better example of transparency's incredible power to drive progress than the food industry.

Today, there is a simmering national debate over the labeling of foods made with genetically modified organisms (GMOs). A law recently enacted in Vermont, for example, requires genetically modified foods to be labeled, starting in July 2016. Likewise, the Whole Foods Market chain has promised to be fully transparent about the use of GMOs in products they sell by 2018. And in April 2015, Chipotle announced it had eliminated GMO ingredients from its food, making it "the first national restaurant chain" to do so. On the other side of the debate, many in the food industry argue that genetically modified foods are safe (and most scientists agree, for what it's worth), rendering any new labeling requirements unnecessary. In addition, there has been a bipartisan effort in Congress to implement a voluntary labeling system that would prohibit state regulations like Vermont's.

But perhaps the most remarkable aspect of today's robust GMO debate is the distance we've traveled when it comes to food safety and transparency. At the beginning of the twentieth century, consumers were at the mercy of the food industry, with little way of protecting themselves against the hazards of unsafe foods. According to the U.S. Food and Drug Administration (FDA):

> Use of chemical preservatives and toxic colors was virtually uncontrolled. Changes from an agricultural to an industrial economy had made it necessary to provide the rapidly increasing city population with food from distant areas. But sanitation was primitive in the light of modern standards. Ice was still the principal means of refrigeration. The great pioneers of bacteriology were just starting their string of victories over infectious diseases. Milk was still unpasteurized. Cows were not tested for tuberculosis.

In the 1880s, a new movement widely supported by women's clubs began demanding food safety reforms. Known as the "pure food" movement, it had as its most influential voice a Dr. Harvey Washington Wiley. As the chief chemist at the U.S. Department of Agriculture, Wiley succeeded in bringing national attention to the need for government oversight and regulation of food. At one point, he even created volunteer "poison squads" to test the effects of foods laced with additives. Federal food safety legislation finally gained enough momentum to make it through Congress in 1906. Not coincidentally, as you may recall from high school, that was the year Upton Sinclair published *The Jungle*, his novel exposing the notoriously noxious practices of the Chicago meatpacking industry. As the *New York Times* recalled a century after the book was published:

> Nothing in *The Jungle* sticks with the reader quite like what went into the sausages. There was the rotting ham that could no longer be sold as ham. There were the rat droppings, rat poison, and whole poisoned rats. Most chilling, there were the unnamed things "in comparison with which a poisoned rat was a tidbit."

Sinclair's disturbing descriptions sparked mass outrage—but not the kind he originally intended. What you might not recall from history class is that Sinclair was a socialist who had set out to expose the poor labor conditions faced by factory workers. In fact, he dedicated *The Jungle* to "the workingmen of America." (In other words, it's probably safe to assume that Sinclair would have a tough time accepting the central argument of this book—that profit can save the planet—though I think he would be thrilled with the working conditions in LEED-certified manufacturing facilities!) But instead of reducing the public's appetite for capitalism, Sinclair simply took away people's appetites. As Sinclair put it, "I aimed at the public's heart, and by accident I hit it in the stomach."

Even though Sinclair missed his intended target, *The Jungle* hit the bull's-eye for the pure food crusade. After the book was published, President Theodore Roosevelt sent his labor commissioner to investigate the conditions in the meatpacking industry, resulting in a report that corroborated Sinclair's claims. In early June 1906, Roosevelt sent the report to Congress, calling its findings "revolting." By the end of the month, Congress had passed two major pieces of legislation: the Federal Meat Inspection Act and the Pure Food and Drug Act. The latter law—commonly known as the Wiley Act—outlawed the mislabeling of food and drugs and effectively established the government oversight of the food industry.

As the swift response to *The Jungle* makes clear, allowing the public to review the contents of what they consume can result in significant institutional change. Of course, that was only the beginning of transparency in the food industry. Over the past century, a series of laws and regulations have created more stringent labeling requirements and safety guidelines. And as evidenced by the debate over GMOs, the crusade for transparency is still happening today.

When it comes to adopting the two new R's, that's a key point. Transparency always leads to more transparency, so even small measures in the near term can result in big, societal shifts in the long run. Just as important, our recent history shows that transparency remains an effective driver of individual *and* institutional changes in behavior.

For instance, the consumption of trans fats took a nosedive in the 2000s, when the FDA began requiring food companies to label products containing them. According to a study by the Centers for Disease Control and Prevention, the amount of trans fats in the blood of white adults declined by 58 percent over the course of the previous decade. That's certainly impressive—but the most remarkable change may have occurred at the institutional level, not the personal one. The Grocery Manufacturers Association has boasted that "food manufacturers have voluntarily lowered the amounts of trans fats in their food products by over 73 percent."

More recently, the FDA announced sweeping rule changes in late 2014—in accordance with the Affordable Care Act— that will require many establishments to include calorie counts on their menus. Once again, early evidence suggests that making it easier for consumers to review the calorie content of their food may influence the choices not just of individuals but of restaurants, too. According to the journal *Health Affairs*, "Large chain restaurants reduced the calories in their new menu items by 60 calories (or 12 percent) from 2012 to 2013, possibly in anticipation of the FDA regulation since no meaningful changes were observed from 2010 to 2011."

It's clear that transparency can be a powerful force for progress. And yet for too long we have failed to apply its power to many consumer products that have the potential to cause extraordinary harm. Think about it this way: Even if you're not counting calories, you probably read the descriptions on a menu before ordering at a restaurant. And if you have a serious food allergy, you definitely don't roll the dice on a dish without reviewing its ingredients. But every day we rely on products without knowing anything about what's in them, risking routine exposure to chemicals that can make us sick.

To be clear, we could not live as we do on this planet without the chemicals that keep us healthy and safe. In fact, some of the most progressive, greenthinking businesses are chemical companies like Dow and BASF, and many of them are members of USGBC. That said, there are many chemicals in consumer products that we know little to nothing about, and that ignorance—as much as the chemicals themselves—is bad for us.

When I was working at Carrier, I brought in the late Danish professor Ole Fanger—one of the world's leading indoor air quality experts—to give a talk. Fanger made a truly terrifying observation that has stuck with me ever since. "What is the first thing Americans do when they find out they are having a baby?" he asked. The answer, of course, is that we spend a huge amount of time and money creating the perfect nursery. We paint the baby's room. We install fresh carpet. We buy a brand-new crib and surround it with new toys. Then we close and lock the windows to keep our newborn safe and snug.

The perfect American nursery, Professor Fanger observed, is actually the perfect gas chamber. The new paint and carpet, the new made-in-China furniture and plastic toys—everything we traditionally put in nurseries is often loaded with chemicals that off-gas for months, if not years. And with the windows closed, there's nowhere for those fumes to go except, as Fanger disturbingly noted, into your baby's lungs.

By contrast, Fanger told us that parents in Denmark take a radically different approach. They strip and sand the floors.

They use nontoxic paints. They might hang a mobile over the crib, but otherwise they keep the room relatively spare. And, he said, they open the windows to keep the fresh air flowing all day long.

While Fanger's illustration was startling to me as a parent, it was downright intimidating as a believer in sustainability. If there can be that many health hazards in one small nursery, just think of the rest of the house!

When my son was little, my wife and I bought a new dresser for his bedroom. But as soon as I put it by his bed, the room began to reek from the formaldehyde, glue, laminate, and particleboard the dresser was made of. So I put the thing in the garage, and I called a friend of mine who was a materials scientist to ask him what I should do about the god-awful smell. He told me that the best thing was to "bake it off." In industrial settings, that means literally putting the offending object in the oven. Of course, that wasn't going to work with my son's dresser. Instead, my friend advised me to leave the thing out on the porch in the hot summer sun for a week. Sure enough, seven days later, the smell was gone. (Mostly.)

Recently, I bought a new car. As I drove off the lot and deeply inhaled that wonderful new car smell, I started to wonder just what that smell could be. I did a little research and found out: noxious chemicals. According to a 2012 report by the Ecology Center, the chemicals used in car interiors "can be harmful when inhaled or ingested and may lead to severe health impacts such as birth defects, learning disabilities, and cancer." The 2011 Mitsubishi Outlander Sport, for instance, was ranked dead last by the Ecology Center due to the bromine, chromium, and lead found in the interior fabric and trim.

Take a moment to look around the room you're sitting in right now (or, if you are lucky enough to be reading this on a beach, take another sip of your margarita and imagine your living room). There is a good chance you're sitting on a couch or a chair treated with flame-retardants that have been linked to a host of health issues, from memory loss to fertility problems. Your carpet could be emitting volatile organic compounds (VOCs) that can lead to throat irritation and headaches. On the other hand, a wood floor isn't necessarily better—all of your wooden furniture could be off-gassing formaldehyde, which is classified as a "human carcinogen." Are you enjoying a cool refreshment while you read? Many of the plastic bottles and containers in your home probably contain Bisphenol A (or BPA), whose effects on human health are still a matter of scientific debate. And that's to say nothing of the chemical-filled products that keep our homes "clean."

In the words of Lisa Jackson, former head of the EPA who now oversees environmental initiatives at Apple, "A child in America today will grow up exposed to more chemicals than any other generation in history." The inescapable truth is that we come into contact with proven hazards and potentially harmful substances every single day—sometimes for hours at a time. But almost none of the products that contain them have a list of ingredients or a warning label plastered on the side. In many cases, the *manufacturers* don't even know what chemicals are in their products, because their suppliers haven't told them.

And here's the really scary part: the Toxic Substances Control Act of 1976—the law meant to protect us from harmful substances in consumer products—is woefully ineffective and outdated. As Dr. Sanjay Gupta, CNN's chief medical correspondent, memorably testified before Congress, the current law essentially treats chemicals like criminal defendants: "innocent until proven guilty." Although companies must notify the EPA before putting a new chemical on the market, they are not required to prove that it's safe. Rather, the burden is on the EPA to demonstrate that the chemical in question poses an "unreasonable risk." If the EPA doesn't make that determination within ninety days—which is not always enough time to collect and analyze data of this sort—the new substance enters the market, our environment, our homes, and our bodies. "As a result, the overwhelming majority of chemicals in use today have never been independently tested for safety," explained the *New York Times* in 2013. "In its history, the EPA has mandated safety testing for only a small percentage of the 85,000 industrial chemicals available for use today. And once chemicals are in use, the burden on the EPA is so high that it has succeeded in banning or restricting only five substances."

Read that one more time. In nearly forty years, the EPA has banned only *five* chemicals out of more than *85,000*.

It's clear that we need to do more to encourage transparency, particularly at a time when toxic partisanship will make it extremely difficult to reach an adequate legislative solution. That's why USGBC made an unprecedented effort to promote transparency with our latest ratings system. In late 2013, we unveiled LEED v4, which—for the very first time—awards points simply for *disclosing* information about the chemicals that building materials contain. Let me be clear: while projects can earn points for avoiding certain toxic substances, they are also rewarded simply for being transparent about them.

As you can probably imagine, this aspect of LEED v4 is controversial. We took some heat from members of the environmental community who couldn't believe that we would call a building "green" even when it contains harmful chemicals. We also took some heat from the chemical companies, which saw this as potentially an unfair level of scrutiny into their products, and one that potentially could negatively impact their industry. But I'm confident that we made the right call, because I know that a little bit of transparency can lead to a lot of sustainability.

Thankfully, USGBC isn't alone in our push for transparency. There's a growing movement to make sustainability reporting more robust. In the building industry, for example, the HPD Collaborative and other nonprofits are pushing for the adoption of Health Product Declarations (HPDs) and Environmental Product Declarations (EPDs). An HPD presents a standardized way to report what's in a building product and its potential health risks, while an EPD does the same for environmental concerns. The idea is simple: make reporting easy to do and standard across the field, and more people and organizations just might start doing it.

Beyond the building industry, Corporate America within the past decade has come to recognize the value of sustainability reporting. According to media and information firm Thomson Reuters, 95 percent of the world's 250 largest companies release a sustainability report of some kind. But these reports are far more valuable to the public—and to investors—if they're comparable. That's why efforts such as the Global Reporting Initiative, the International Integrated Reporting Committee, and the Sustainability Accounting Standards Board are trying to ensure that, on a national and international level, corporate sustainability reports are evaluated not in a vacuum, but in context.

Sustainability reporting at the corporate level is terrific, but it's hardly enough. We need better mechanisms to review and report at the *product* level. So how can we convince the private sector to embrace the fourth and fifth R's? Well, I believe the first step is simply to raise awareness—and that's a marketing challenge, not a technical one.

We all know how to tell if something is recyclable. We just look for that familiar symbol, three arrows forming a triangle in a Mobius loop. If you pick up the nearest bottle or can, odds are that there is only one symbol other than the brand logo— it's recognizable, it's unobtrusive, and its meaning is clear.

Now, imagine if there were *two* immediately recognizable symbols on the consumer products you handle each and every day—one that tells you whether a product is recyclable and another that tells you whether it's *reviewable*. Imagine a universal symbol indicating that a product's manufacturer has disclosed its contents and made them available for scrutiny by the public. Right alongside the Mobius loop, I want you to imagine a global symbol of transparency: a magnifying glass.

Just because a product is recyclable doesn't mean that it's not harmful. Moreover, it doesn't matter if a product is recyclable if we aren't planning to throw it away. So while the recycling symbol is great, it doesn't tell us anything about our electronic devices, our furniture, or our clothes and the impact they have on our environment and, yes, on our bodies. The magnifying glass would be more than a mere symbol. Just as the Mobius loop encourages people to consider the impact of their trash, the magnifying glass would encourage people to consider the impact of items that they are exposed to constantly and keep for years at a time.

In my fantasy, you would be able to turn over your iPhone and find, somewhere below the Apple logo, a small magnifying glass. Then you could go to Apple's website and find a list of the materials used to make the phone. The magnifying glass would be on the soles of your shoes and the tags on your couch cushions, and the contents of those products would be easily reviewable on the websites of the companies that make them.

Come on, Rick, you might be thinking. *What good would that do? I'm not a chemist, and neither are you.* But consumers don't need to know the periodic table to benefit from companies being transparent about the chemicals they use to make consumer products. That's because the mere act of disclosure, as we've seen in the food industry over the past hundred years, will drive change—and profit.

For instance, let's say Company X is making Product Y with a suspected carcinogen, Chemical Z. And let's say that consumers begin to demand transparency for consumer products. They'll be more likely, in that case, to buy a widget if it has a magnifying glass stamped on it. In a world where consumers value and demand transparency, you better believe that Company X is going to eliminate Chemical Z from Product Y so it doesn't have to explain its use of a potentially cancer-causing ingredient. And that will be a very good thing—even if you don't know what the heck Chemical Z is, let alone how to spell it.

A magnifying glass on consumer products might seem like a pipe dream, but it's no less likely than calorie counts on restaurant menus would have been not long ago. In reality, it's a small change that doesn't even require legislation. It simply allows manufacturers to opt-in to the fourth and fifth R's. Furthermore, there is a compelling reason for companies to embrace this kind of voluntary disclosure. In the same way that green building is profitable, transparency is a good for business—and some companies are already proving it.

In 2001, Eric Ryan and Adam Lowry founded the soap and cleaning supplies company Method Home. In an industry long dominated by large corporations, they were convinced that a brand committed to environmentally friendly products and modern design could provide a fresh alternative that consumers would value. They were right. Within five years, Method was generating more than $30 million in annual revenue. Incredibly, the company's revenues ballooned to more than $100 million in 2012.

Method's motto is "people against dirty"—and the company is applying it to more than dish soap and detergent. In April 2015, Method opened a new plant in Chicago that is the first LEED Platinum soap factory in the world. The company is also offering customers a clear look at the contents of their products. At the top of Method's website is a tab labeled "Beyond the Bottle," which provides a link to a page listing every ingredient that Method uses. There you can find a simple chart that identifies each ingredient, along with "what it does" (e.g., moisturizer, colorant) and an "environmental + health summary" (e.g. "biodegrades readily; derived from canola oil; not irritating to the skin"). Near the top of the ingredients page, some information labeled "Transparency" appears under—you guessed it—a magnifying glass.

———

Let me close this chapter with a story about something for which, like many Americans, I have a deep and abiding passion.

Bacon.

Applegate Farms opened its doors in 1987 as a small smokehouse in New Jersey dedicated to producing nitrate-free meat. Sure, Applegate's bacon was pretty darn tasty, but *all* bacon tastes great. Which is why the trajectory of Applegate's business over the past three decades is particularly remarkable.

Applegate started by asking, "What if you weren't afraid to read the ingredients on a hot dog package?" It has built its brand around being transparent about its ingredients and processes, and today it is the largest natural and organic meat company in America, with sales projected to be $340 million in 2015. You can find Applegate products in small specialty food stores but also in big chains like Whole Foods, Stop & Shop, and A&P. Applegate is even transparent about the impact of its product on the planet, which is why the company's founder, Stephen McDonnell, encourages people to eat less meat.

In May 2015, Hormel bought Applegate for $775 million. Applegate is not profitable *despite* its transparent business practices—it's profitable entirely *because* of them. (On behalf of organic bacon fans everywhere, I sure hope Hormel keeps up the transparency that has won Applegate so many loyal customers.) In a world in which sustainability is profitable, Applegate's success is proof positive that transparency is the private sector's best friend.

If we're serious about creating a sustainable planet, then we need to recognize that consumption isn't necessarily the enemy. The enemy, instead, is unthinking and unknowing consumption. The enemy is the opacity of the ingredients and processing methods of products we routinely use. If corporations leverage reporting as a marketing and brand-building opportunity—and if consumers and governments embrace reviewing to make healthier decisions and smarter regulations—the world will be a far more sustainable place. If you ask me, nothing is more *transparent* than that.

8

ENVIRONMENTALISM 2.0

"Our choice is not whether change will come,
but whether we can guide that change in the
service of our ideal and toward a social order
shaped to the needs of all our people."
—*Robert F. Kennedy*

MY HOMETOWN OF SYRACUSE is not far from Seneca Falls, the birthplace of the women's rights movement. I remember learning about the movement when I was a kid—about Wesleyan Chapel, Elizabeth Cady Stanton, and the Women's Rights Convention. It's hard to imagine there was a time in this country when women had no rights, when they couldn't vote, when they were seen as property. But in 1848, folks got together in a little town by a lake in upstate New York and began a movement that would change America and the world.

I've always revered the great social movements of the nineteenth and twentieth centuries. I was in third grade when Dr. Martin Luther King Jr. gave his "I Have a Dream" speech, and I remember a year later when President Lyndon Johnson signed the Civil Rights Act into law. I was in high school when the Stonewall protests brought the LGBT rights movement to the national stage. I had just graduated from business school when gay rights activists marched on Washington in the midst of the AIDS crisis of the 1980s.

I don't know if all this makes me sound old. To me, it makes these incredible social movements feel recent.

I think about them when contemplating the future of environmentalism. On the one hand, our movement to build a sustainable world is very different from the other movements for freedom and equality in American history. Environmental degradation is a cause of social inequality, that's for sure, but environmental injustice is a subtler form of discrimination. The enemies aren't (usually) misogynists, racists, or homophobes. The enemy is everywhere and nowhere; it's the infrastructure of modern, industrial life.

Obvious differences aside, however, environmentalism does have a tremendous amount to learn from social movements past and present, and one critical lesson in particular:

Being right isn't enough.

The women's rights, civil rights, labor rights, and gay rights movements all were—and are—on the side of the angels. From our vantage point, it seems obvious that these social movements prevailed. It's unthinkable in today's world that people were once denied the right to attend public school, to be hired for a job, to vote, or even to sit at a lunch counter because of their race. It's impossible to understand how child labor and unsafe working conditions were once not only acceptable in America, but commonplace. It's hard to believe that our country's laws categorically denied (and continue to deny!) equal rights to its citizens based on their gender or their sexual preference. We look back at our history and see obvious injustices that made these movements right and necessary.

However, social movements don't win because they're on the right side of history. They win because they're *effective*. Nonviolent protest, union organizing, political, judicial, and economic activism—these were the brilliantly effective strategies that the great social movements devised and deployed to prevail in the face of powerful, cruel, and oftentimes violent opposition.

Today, environmentalists struggle to understand how society can so callously and knowingly poison the air and the water. We can't grasp why—given the dire consequences of environmental degradation for human and planetary health—sustainability has been an occasional afterthought instead of a universal core value. We can't explain why—given that 74 percent of Americans (and 51 percent of Republicans!) want the federal government to address climate change—movement in Congress has stalled. There's no real question that sustainability *should* be embraced throughout society. Environmentalism has history, morality, science, public opinion, and even the Pope on its side!

So what's missing?

The central insights of the environmental movement are deeply, fundamentally virtuous. But look at the *state* of our movement. Look at all we have failed to achieve. Yes, environmentalism is righteous, but our tactics have become obsolete. The elements of a young social movement—an inspirational idea, a call for change, a sense of moral urgency—are no longer enough to carry the environmental movement forward. Just like other great American social movements, we have to devise and deploy strategies that will lead us to victory. We have to be more effective. We have to win.

WE. HAVE. TO. WIN!

When the women's rights movement was agitating for suffrage, its supporters battled in the knowledge that even if they fell short, their daughters and sons would pick up the struggle for them. When the brave activists of the civil rights movement marched together, they walked with a sure sense that, as Dr. King would say, the "arc of the moral universe" was bending, however slowly, "toward justice." Today, the visionaries of the gay rights movement are fighting for equal protection and recognition under the law. They've won historic, heroic battles, most recently in the Supreme Court, and there are more battles to come. But even if they fail one day, one week, or one year, there will always be another day, another week, and another year to continue the campaign for true equality.

The brave souls who fight for social justice know, in other words, that their first chance at victory is never their last. But today, the environmental movement does not have that comfort. Instead, we have this challenge:

We are almost out of time.

This is not to say that the environmental movement is in any way more urgent than these other historic movements for justice and inequality. It's only to say that, in this case, our window is rapidly closing. Soon, the catastrophic effects of climate change will be irreversible. In January 2014, the United Nations issued a report finding that if we do not take significant steps toward reducing global carbon emissions over the next fifteen years, climate change will be all but impossible to mitigate with existing technology. In May 2014, the White House released the National Climate Assessment, in which scientists state, "Climate change, once considered an issue for a distant future, has moved firmly into the present."

This is sobering news. Our children and our successors in the environmental movement won't be able to pick up where we left off. Instead, they'll be forced to deal with the horrible consequences of our failure. The ice caps are melting, the seas are rising, the world is warming, and pollution is mounting as I write this sentence and as you read this book.

That's why the environmental movement as we know it must come to an end.

The old environmentalism has brought us this far. But we have *so* much farther to go, and we need to get there *fast*. That's why we must totally and completely redefine environmentalism around the idea that I've established in this book—that sustainability is profitable. We need a brand-new environmental movement to catapult us to the next level. We need a movement that harnesses the incredible power of the profit motive instead of struggling in vain to suppress it. Because the truth is, enterprise is environmentalism's only hope.

Once upon a time, we saved the planet.

At first, nobody knew there was a problem. An invisible gas, emitted by everyday consumer goods, was contaminating our atmosphere and threatening the future of life on Earth. Slowly but surely, the empirical evidence grew until it was undeniable.

Something had to be done.

The United States government started with domestic regulation, but that wasn't enough. This was a global problem that no single nation could solve. Soon there was an international treaty that established an ambitious goal. The United States signed on, as did 196 other countries, including every single member of the United Nations.

This global compact worked. The damage caused by the harmful gas was slowed, then halted, and then reversed.

This might sound like an environmentalist's utopian daydream, a fantasy of what the world *should* do in response to the imminent threat of climate change. But this isn't a work of fiction. It's history—*recent* history.

The pollutant in question wasn't carbon dioxide, though.

It was chlorofluorocarbons, or CFCs—released by air conditioners, refrigerators, fire extinguishers, aerosol cans, and countless other consumer products. In 1974, the University of California's Mario Molina and F. Sherwood Rowland identified the threat of CFCs in the upper atmosphere, where they break apart into smaller pieces, including the element chlorine. Molina and Rowland discovered that this chlorine was devouring the ozone layer, which protects the Earth from deadly ultraviolet radiation. No ozone layer means no plants, no insects, no bacteria, no animals, no people—in other words, a planet that looks more like Mars than Earth. CFCs were depleting the ozone layer with astonishing speed, the researchers found; just one atom of chlorine from CFCs can wipe out 100,000 molecules of ozone.

I guess bad things come in small packages, too.

By the late 1970s, the EPA issued a rule banning the use of CFCs in aerosol sprays. Unfortunately, this didn't stop or even slow the production of CFCs, which continued to rise into the 1980s. Then, in 1985, the British Antarctic Survey made a frightening discovery: a third of the ozone layer had apparently vanished between 1972 and 1982, and CFCs were the cause. At this point, the science was indisputable, and the danger undeniable. And then, something amazing happened— something we haven't seen happen since.

The world acted.

Kind of like in the movie *Independence Day*, but without the aliens.

In 1987, the world came together to sign the Montreal Protocol, which required the private sector to cut CFC production in half within ten years. When new evidence revealed that a more drastic solution was required, the protocol was updated to stop *all* CFC production in the developed world by 1996. Despite industry's early protests that CFCs were a necessary and irreplaceable component of the consumer products they manufactured, businesses were able to find new substitutes and workarounds to get CFCs out of our atmosphere.

Long story short, it worked. According to the EPA, chlorine levels in the stratosphere reached their highest levels in the late 1990s, and they've been steadily declining ever since. The ozone layer is now on its way to a full recovery.

Needless to say, the battle to ban CFCs was perhaps the most important environmental victory in world history. And I'm proud to have been part of it. In fact, I was named the first director of environmental marketing at Carrier precisely as a result of our need to address the global CFC threat. This is how I cut my teeth in sustainability!

Unfortunately, times have changed since then. Fast-forward twenty years to the recent fight between environmentalists and the business community over the Keystone XL pipeline.

In 2008, energy company TransCanada decided to build off an existing Canadian oil pipeline called Keystone to connect Alberta's oil sands to Nebraska, and ultimately to refineries on the Gulf Coast. Just a few months later, President Obama took office, and along with it the responsibility for approving the expansion of the pipeline through the United States. The environmental movement, led by many of its most prominent organizations and voices, mobilized an incredible, historic response. The *New York Times* reported that their activism initially succeeded in pushing President Obama to put off his decision about the pipeline until after the 2012 elections. In 2013, activists staged one of the largest protests in the history of the environmental movement, featuring tens of thousands of people marching in Washington, DC. And in 2014, nearly four hundred Keystone XL protesters were arrested outside the White House. One of the protesters told Reuters, "If the Democratic Party wants to keep our vote, they better make sure President Obama rejects that pipeline."

Meanwhile, the U.S. Department of State had undertaken an extensive review of the pipeline's effect on the environment and the climate. On January 31, 2014, the State Department released the final version of its report, which suggests that if the pipeline were built, it would not significantly increase carbon pollution. But then, a judge in Nebraska blocked the pipeline, causing the State Department to hold its decision until the legal situation is resolved.

Whatever—and whenever—the final outcome, the fight over Keystone XL exemplifies a larger problem. It's true that every time we build a new pipeline or invest in fossil fuel extraction, we delay the badly needed twenty-first-century "Manhattan project" that will bring renewable energy technologies into the mainstream marketplace. That said, as someone who cares passionately not just about the environmental movement but also about its success, the movement's activism around Keystone XL seriously bothered me. Sure, it was a convenient focal point for a lot of frustrated energy and anger about our government's failure to enact a meaningful response to the climate crisis. But was it the right focus? History will answer that question, but the facts today aren't encouraging. If you ask me, the only encouraging aspect of the Keystone XL demonstrations is that they prove the environmental movement still has plenty of fight in it.

But let's remember that the fight against climate change isn't a fight against *pipelines*. It's a fight against *carbon emissions*. And by defeating the XL extension, will environmentalists have slowed, stopped, or reversed carbon emissions? The answer is, resoundingly, *no*. The relative impact of stopping the Keystone XL pipeline would be only a drop in the bucket. As the *New York Times* reported, carbon emissions connected to Keystone "would amount to less than 1 percent of United States greenhouse gas emissions, and an infinitesimal slice of the global total."

More to the point, with the Keystone XL pipeline in limbo, oil producers looked for other ways to get their product to market. And they found a good one: trains. According to news agency Reuters, "oil-train traffic has surged at least 42-fold since 2009." While the Obama administration was buying time evaluating Keystone, the news website Slate reported that rail transportation capacity for oil increased by more than half of the Keystone pipeline's expected capacity. In fact, rail companies have been so successful meeting the transport needs of oil producers that one expert told Slate, "The pipeline guys have got to be scared."

It's hard to consider these two stories—the historic effort to marshal global action to save the ozone layer, and the unending fight a couple of decades later over the construction of a single pipeline—and not see that something fundamental has changed.

The environmental movement has certainly grown in size, power, and influence since the 1970s, and today it has many talented and dedicated lobbyists on Capitol Hill. In fact, the protests over Keystone XL show just how much the environmental movement's capacity for activism has increased over the years. Today, the movement has more members, more funding, and its backers are as full of energy and passion as ever. And needless to say, its overall goal—building a more sustainable world—has never been more urgent.

But the hard truth is that the movement is failing. Yes, there have been important victories: tighter vehicle efficiency standards and more investments in renewable energy nationally, and renewable portfolio standards and cap-and-trade systems at the state and regional levels. But the big battles? The environmental movement has been losing them. Decisively.

The Kyoto Protocol is one famous example. The protocol—formulated in Kyoto, Japan, and agreed to in principle by the United States in 1997—capped greenhouse gas emissions for developed nations. But the U.S. is one of only a handful of countries never to ratify the treaty. Why? Because the U.S. Senate at the time was convinced that it was choosing between the environment and economic growth. And it wasn't even a close call. According to Benjamin Kline in his history of the environmental movement, *First Along the River*, even before the draft of Kyoto had been settled, the Senate voted "that the United States should not be a signatory to any protocol that did not include binding targets and timetables for developing as well as industrialized nations or 'would result in serious harm to the economy of the United States.'"

Just over a decade later, in December 2009, the nations of the world met again in Copenhagen. Again, despite promises, optimism, and plenty of good intentions, the Copenhagen negotiations foundered. How did it all go wrong in Copenhagen? It's no mystery. Once again, the idea that environmental goals stood in the way of growth was an insurmountable obstacle in the negotiations. *Foreign Policy* magazine summed it up nicely: "If there is one ideological commitment that unites nations and people around the world in the early twenty-first century, it is that GDP growth is non-negotiable."

We glimpsed a ray of hope in 2014 when President Obama announced a major climate deal with China. This historic agreement was the first time China has committed to capping carbon, and because our two countries are responsible for nearly half of all greenhouse gas emissions, it has the potential to create a significant impact for years to come. But it also provided a glum reminder of how the environmental movement has failed of late. Shortly after the China climate deal was made public by the president, it was denounced by Republicans. Senator Mitch McConnell, the Republican leader in the Senate, said the deal would "increase the squeeze on middle-class families" and "ensure higher utility rates and far fewer jobs." Over in the House of Representatives, Republican speaker John Boehner called it another of the president's "job-crushing policies."

Of course, it's not just international deals that have fallen through or come under fire. Domestically, the environmental movement has continued to suffer major blows on Capitol Hill. Look no further than the failure of cap-and-trade. In 2009, the House voted 219–212 to advance a bill known as Waxman-Markey that would have set ambitious renewable energy targets and created a new regime of emissions caps and tradable permits. The ideas in that bill had some bipartisan support and even resembled amendments to the Clean Air Act signed by George H. W. Bush in 1990. The environmental movement was behind it, and at least one major political party and the White House were lending their support.

But after Waxman-Markey passed the House by this razor-thin margin, the Senate did . . . nothing. No vote. Not even a filibuster. The bill simply died, and when Senate negotiations over a potential substitute fell apart, so did the hope of a legislative solution to catastrophic climate change.

There are two ways to look at these enormous, recent

failures of the environmental movement to marshal the kind of effective policy response to climate change that we saw during the CFC crisis in the 1980s. The first way is one I hear a lot about in the environmental movement: *We lost the fight because we didn't work hard enough, fight fiercely enough, march far enough, or protest loudly enough.* But there's another way to look at it—a more accurate and, I believe, more productive way: *We lost the fight because we allowed business and growth to become our opponents.* In our attempts to spur action at Kyoto and Copenhagen, we were effectively setting ourselves up to go head to head with global business. In the fight for cap-and-trade, people assumed—or were persuaded by the environmental movement's opponents—that we were going after their jobs. These are fights that environmentalists will lose every day of the week and twice on Sunday.

Environmentalists picked the wrong opponent because too many of us have a worldview that no longer suits the times, and many think—wrongly—that in order to be an environmentalist we have to subscribe this worldview. But the environmental movement's enemy isn't business, industrial activity, jobs, or economic growth; the enemy is environmental degradation and climate change. For too long, environmentalists have continued to buy into the idea that we need to defeat the former to defeat the latter.

This zero-sum worldview has finally reached its sell-by date. Both domestically and internationally, choosing between a sustainable future and a prosperous one doesn't provide a useful framework to guide action or public policy. That old way of thinking has led us to the sad status quo in which we find ourselves today: a world without a healthy environment *or* a strong economy.

In other words, *everybody is losing.*

In the introduction to this book, I showed how environmentalists have traditionally treated the business community as an antagonist—and with good reason. For a long time, industry *was* the opponent. And the tripartite tactic of agitation, legislation, and regulation was incredibly effective in putting points on the board. But today, the game has changed—completely. Sustainability is now profitable. And that means environmental organizations need a new plan of attack. Today, greenthink offers a different three-part strategy that is far more effective, disruptive, and transformative. It's a model that USGBC and others have pioneered. It's proven, it's effective, and it's ready for prime time.

The first part of this new strategy is simple: *connect the dots between sustainability and profitability.* To put it a different way, the most successful environmental organizations today work *with* business to show them how much money they can save—and/or make—by transitioning to sustainable business practices.

One of the best examples of this tactic was perhaps the very first attempt at deploying it. The Environmental Defense

Fund (EDF) was founded in 1967 with a mission that's right there in its name: to defend the environment. The organization has racked up some huge wins over the years, including its successful effort to push through the 1990 amendments to the Clean Air Act. That same year, EDF struck up a revolutionary partnership with McDonald's, which became a test case for a new kind of environmental activism.

McDonald's has served "billions and billions" of people around the world. In the process, it's also created billions and billions of pounds of waste. Every Happy Meal, every order of supersized fries, and every extra-large soda comes in a familiar McDonald's container emblazoned with the golden arches. For a long time, those containers were made out of polystyrene—a.k.a. Styrofoam—which is terrible for the environment and can stay in our landfills for centuries without breaking down. This is the stuff that was used to gently enclose your Big Mac in its clamshell container, until EDF sat down with McDonald's and posed the question: Was this packaging efficient? It was an ingenious thing to focus on, because "efficient" meant two things simultaneously. For EDF it meant: Was the packaging *environmentally* efficient? While McDonald's was open to pondering that question, the company was also interested in another one: Was its packaging *economically* efficient? EDF helped McDonald's see something amazing: they were the same question. They also had the same answer: an overwhelming "no."

With EDF's help, McDonald's changed its packaging—

for the better, and for good. Instead of polystyrene boxes, McDonald's started serving burgers and sandwiches in paper-based wrapping, and the company also started incorporating postconsumer recycled content into its paper products. All in all, over the next decade, McDonald's "eliminated more than 300 million pounds of packaging, recycled 1 million tons of corrugated boxes, and reduced waste by 30 percent." The best part is that this positive change didn't cost McDonald's a single penny—in fact, it saves them $6 million each year.

Since that breakthrough partnership with McDonald's, EDF has developed other programs that connect the dots between profitability and sustainability. In 2008, for instance, the organization created the EDF Climate Corps, which matches teams of MBA students with large corporations to develop strategies that reduce waste, keep greenhouse gases out of the air, and—most important from the perspective of their private-sector partners—save millions of dollars.

In the years since EDF pioneered this strategy, other organizations have followed suit. The best ones have taken it a step further. First, they demonstrate to private-sector partners how profitable sustainability can be. And second, they *develop systems to make it easier for corporations and consumers to do the right thing for the planet.*

USGBC's LEED rating system is a great example of making it easier for the private sector to adopt sustainable building practices and materials. But one of the original nonprofits to deploy this second strategy was none other than the World

Wildlife Fund (WWF). Don't be fooled by their cuddly panda bear logo. Sure, WWF is intently focused on conservation. And yes, WWF was founded in 1961, making it one of the world's oldest environmental organizations. But it was also among the first to recognize the need to constructively engage with and leverage the private sector to protect animals, people, and the planet.

WWF believes that "the power of the global marketplace can and must be transformed into a force for conservation." And the organization has created a number of incredible industry certification programs that have done just that. A great example is the Marine Stewardship Council (MSC), which WWF and Unilever cofounded in 1996 to certify sustainably caught seafood. Today, according to WWF, "nearly 15,000 seafood products with over $3 billion in annual sales bear the MSC label." More recently, in 2009, WWF cofounded the International Seafood Sustainability Foundation (ISSF) with eight canned tuna companies to promote conservation practices that benefit the environment and industry. ISSF now includes 26 private sector partners and covers 75 percent of the canned tuna industry. WWF has also cofounded similar industry partnerships that are making it easier for producers of sugar, soy, and palm oil to implement sustainable farming methods. Some of these partnerships even create incentives for sustainability. And WWF is not alone.

I've been working with the Natural Resources Defense Council for years. Not only is the NRDC a great organization, but it also has been exemplary in its willingness to pursue partnerships with the private sector. And none of these partnerships has been more exciting (in my opinion) than the NRDC's work to bring sustainability to sports.

What started in 2003 as a partnership with one team, the Philadelphia Eagles, and in 2005 grew to include a partnership with one whole league, Major League Baseball, has now become an incredible, widespread movement. As of today, the NRDC is partnered with every major sports league in North America, including the NBA, the NHL, and the NFL. Within each of these leagues, there are stories of incredible sustainability success. In a single year, basketball's Miami Heat saved $1.6 million through green initiatives and better energy consumption (including a LEED-certified arena!), and in the process gained $1 million in corporate sponsorship from companies interested in the team's new green efforts. Between 2006 and 2011, baseball's Seattle Mariners saved $1.5 million on utilities bills and have reduced greenhouse gas emissions by 21.2 million pounds a year.

No matter who you root for, it's hard not to be a fan of the NRDC. The organization is enabling leagues, teams, and venues to evaluate their own consumption using the NRDC's Green Advisor program. Rather than battle the sports industry with pleas and protests, the NRDC is proving that business and nonprofits can play on the same team.

Environmental organizations like EDF have pioneered the incredibly successful strategy of working with industry to make the connection between sustainability and profitability a real and meaningful one. And others, including WWF, the NRDC, and USGBC, are going a step further by implementing private-sector rating systems, partnerships, and programs that make better environmental outcomes cheaper and easier. This is how today's environmental organizations must operate to meaningfully and measurably move the ball toward the goal line.

But the new environmentalism has to be bigger than the world of nonprofits—much bigger. Sure, environmental organizations need to partner with businesses, but some of the most effective environmental organizations you could possibly imagine *are* businesses.

In 2007, Eben Bayer and Gavin McIntyre were seniors at Rensselaer Polytechnic Institute in Troy, New York, when Bayer submitted a class project made out of mushrooms—a disk of sustainable "insulation" he had grown in a jar in his basement. Another teacher might have been upset about this homegrown homework, but Professor Burt Swersey wasn't upset—he was excited. He told the *New Yorker*,

> [Bayer] takes this thing out of his pocket, and it's white, this amazing piece of insulation that had been *grown*, without hydrocarbons, with almost no energy used. The stuff could be made with almost any waste materials—rice husks, cotton wastes, stuff farmers throw away, stuff they have no market for—and it

wouldn't take away from anybody's food supply, and it could be made anywhere from local materials, so you could cut down on transportation costs. And it would be completely biodegradable! What more could you want?

Talk about a fun guy. (Get it?)

With Professor Swersey's help, Bayer and McIntyre started a company called Ecovative. After years of perfecting their craft, they discovered that their mushroom-based product can perform just as well—and cost about the same to produce—as petrochemical plastics like polystyrene. The difference is, Ecovative's Mushroom Packaging is 100 percent compostable and sustainable. More than that, the company has turned a waste stream into something that has tremendous commercial value. And other companies and investors have taken notice. Today, Ecovative is doing very big things, like raising millions of dollars in venture capital to perfect and expand its operations—and winning a number of awards along the way. In 2012, Ecovative entered into a partnership with Sealed Air, the Fortune 500 company best known as the makers of Bubble Wrap. The start-up's customers have also included companies like Dell and Crate & Barrel.

Let's be perfectly clear. Bayer and McIntyre are ardent environmentalists. I don't know these guys personally, but I wouldn't be surprised if, like many of us, they wear their organic food, hybrid vehicle, and recycling merit badges with pride. But as much as Ecovative's founders are obsessed with sustainability, they don't want to be the next Rachel Carson. As Bayer told the *New Yorker*, "We want to be the Dow or DuPont of this century."

Ecovative's goals are *business* goals. Their methods are *business* methods. In years past, environmental organizations might have tried simply to ban polystyrene or Styrofoam. Today, Ecovative is working instead to replace it with something far better, by competing in the marketplace with a truly sustainable product. And it's winning accolades, fame, business, and, oh yeah, money.

Ecovative is one of many companies across America and around the world that are pursuing environmentalism through entrepreneurism and achieving incredible results. Companies like Method, Seventh Generation, and Honest Company are taking natural cleaning products into big chain stores like Whole Foods and Target. TerraCycle has taken trash, such as chip bags and juice boxes, and turned it into trendy products like lunchboxes and backpacks that are sold in Walmart stores across the country. And that's just to name a few. Patagonia's CEO Yvon Chouinard put it well: "Every time we've made a decision that's right for the planet, it's made us more money." To put it in a slightly different way, and in way that should tantalize would-be environmental entrepreneurs: every time money changes hands is an opportunity to do something right for the planet.

Big companies have realized this, and they're starting to

educate their employees. For example, since UTC's Carrier business launched its Distinguished Sustainability Lecture Series in 2011, nearly three thousand people have attended twenty-five events in seventeen cities across thirteen developing countries. And helping these leaders in other countries greenthink unlocks the potential for action at a much larger scale. As Geraud Darnis, president and CEO of UTC Building and Industrial Systems, explained,

> UTC is a Fortune 50 company. We have a responsibility to act like one, and education is a core value at UTC. This program is one where we can give back in our international communities—by inspiring new green building leaders who will act on their newfound knowledge in ways that benefit all of us who want a more sustainable way forward.

But UTC isn't the only entity that needs to act like a Fortune 50 company—environmentalists do, too. This is the third new tactic the environmental movement must embrace: Just as UTC's employees and customers are learning the tools of sustainability, *it's time environmentalists started learning the ways of business.*

Nonprofits will always play a critical role in our movement, there's no question about that. But no environmentalist should be shy about pursuing his or her passion through the private sector. It's why I encourage so many young people to go to business school, because a career in the private sector doesn't mean selling out. Just the opposite—it can mean playing a bigger role in realizing our sustainable future.

Every year at Greenbuild—USGBC's annual green building conference and expo—we give out several leadership awards. In 2012, we recognized a brilliant, charismatic, and all-around wonderful guy named Steve Saunders.

Steve, a businessman from Irving, Texas, got his start in HVAC systems—a great line of work when you live in blistering Texas, but not always an environmentally friendly enterprise. Over the past fifteen years, however, Steve's business has expanded to incorporate green rating systems and design principles, including LEED. Today, two of Steve's companies—U.S.-EcoLogic and TexEnergy Solutions—are the biggest residential energy efficiency and green building consultancies in the world.

Most of Steve's customers aren't environmentalists, though. In fact, when Steve pitches his companies' services to Texas home builders and developers, environmental concerns rarely come up. "I talk to people about how they can make money," Steve says. "I don't talk to them about how they can save the world. That's their business."

But his business *is* a world-saving one. Steve's companies have helped build and certify more than 43,000 ENERGY

STAR homes and 24,000 green apartment units. That translates to more than 141 million square feet, or more than fifty-one Empire State Buildings' worth of space. On top of that, U.S.-EcoLogic and TexEnergy Solutions are together responsible for 20 percent of all LEED-certified housing on Earth, making them the single largest LEED for Homes provider.

If you ask me, Steve is one of the most effective environmentalists anywhere in the world today. Yes, he lives in Texas. Yes, he runs a big business. Yes, he has a deep drawl, listens to country music, and makes a mean barbecue. But tell me: Who wrote the rule that you can't be a red-state environmentalist? Who said environmentalists can't wear business suits? Where is it written in stone that pillaging the Earth is the only way to make a buck?

For years, my message to the business community has been that sustainability is profitable. But the flip side is equally important for the future of the environmental movement and the future of the planet, and today's environmental leaders and activists must hear that message just as clearly:

Profitability is sustainable.

I'm not asking die-hard environmentalists to compromise their most sacred values. I'm not asking them to be any less passionate or committed to the cause of saving the planet and improving the health and well-being of our communities and the people who live, work, play, and learn in them. I'm not suggesting that we wave a white flag to the industries that have spent decades decimating our land and poisoning our water.

All I'm asking of my friends in the environmental movement is this:

Don't distrust the profit motive—*leverage it.*

Don't fear the private sector—*partner with it.*

Don't ignore the marketplace—*embrace it.*

And, more than anything else . . .

Don't waste this opportunity.

The game has changed. The ground has shifted. The time is now.

Building a new environmental movement will require the very same values and skills that made the environmental movement of the past so successful in *its* time. The new environmental movement will require hard work, dedication, idealism, and passion. And yes, it will involve a good bit of righteous indignation.

We still need these things in droves. But one thing we must discard is our deep-seated and disastrous misconception that enterprise is always and inherently bad. The new environmental movement requires a new perspective. If we want to succeed as a movement, it's time to embrace the world of business. If we want to succeed as a movement, it's time to be both right *and* effective. If we want to succeed as a movement, it's time to channel the incredible energy and power of environmentalism into a private-sector force for positive, global change.

In environmentalism 2.0, business isn't the enemy—it's the means by which we can achieve our righteous ends.

A SPEAR
IN THE CHEST

*"We are all part of the continuum of
humanity and life. We will have lived our
brief span and either helped or hurt that
continuum and the Earth that sustains all life.
It's that simple. Which will it be?"*

—*Ray Anderson*

WHEN CHARLES DARWIN WROTE his world-changing book,
On the Origin of Species By Means of Natural Selection, he provided a simple explanation for the astounding complexity of
life on Earth: Nature selects and reproduces the traits best
suited for a species' survival. Some adapt to their surroundings

and thrive. Others fail to adapt and die out. Adaptation isn't a conscious process, of course. Fish didn't decide to grow legs or lungs, and chimps didn't decide to grow bigger brains. Natural selection is the result of many forces, from climatic and environmental changes, to hungry predators, to random genetic mutations that every now and again result in an evolutionary leg up for the next generation.

"Survival of the fittest" has long been applied to the cutthroat world of business. But few people fully appreciate the incredible implications of this idea in today's rapidly changing economic ecosystem. Corporations are being forced to adapt to a new economic environment shaped by climate change and more than a century of industrial pollution. Environmental degradation has become a measurable drag on corporate profits and national economic growth. Consumers are increasingly rewarding companies that offer sustainable products. In short, sustainability has become profitable. In this new economic ecosystem, survival of the *fittest* means survival of the *greenest*. For the private sector, natural selection means *selecting nature*.

The genetic code of businesses is undergoing a dramatic evolution, from a single strand of profit to the double helix of profit and planet. Macroeconomic forces are driving countless companies toward sustainability. Some are on the cutting edge of this economic evolution. Others are moving, slowly but surely, in the direction of sustainable survival. Many have not yet even begun the process of adaptation. A large percentage of these will fail to evolve at all. They'll become the fossils of the fossil fuel age.

There's no question that our evolution to a sustainable economy is under way. But, as the climate clock keeps ticking, it's time to grapple with a different question:

Will we evolve fast enough?

I wrote this book because the answer, today, is "no."

We're on a collision course with catastrophic climate change. Forget about melting glaciers. I'm talking about *economic* meltdown. What happens to Nestlé or General Mills when permanent droughts devastate global agriculture? What happens to Prudential or Berkshire Hathaway—two of the world's largest insurance holding companies—when faced with an onslaught of extreme weather events and unprecedented coastal flooding? What happens to blue chip corporations like Coca-Cola and PepsiCo when water shortages send the beverage industry into a tailspin? What happens to the stock market when corporate profits plunge due to resource scarcity? What happens to the American labor market when the global economy enters a post–climate change environmental depression? And most important, what happens to our kids and our grandkids when these scenarios play out?

I don't want to discover the answers to any of these questions. No one does. We don't have the generations' worth of time necessary to let economic natural selection run its course. That's why we need something more than sustainable evolution. We need a sustainable *revolution*. And revolutions, of course, need leaders.

In 1973, a young entrepreneur named Ray Anderson founded a carpet company in LaGrange, Georgia. Ray had spent fourteen years in the carpet business, and he had a hunch that modular carpeting—which was easier to install and remove— was the future of office furnishing. He was right.

Ray started his business with fifteen employees and a group of investors. By 1978, sales hit $11 million. In the years to follow, the company grew, went public, and expanded abroad. By the mid-1990s, Ray's company—Interface—was the biggest modular carpet manufacturer in the world, with revenues nearing $1 billion, a sales presence in more than one hundred countries, and nearly two dozen factories on four continents.

In 1994, Ray read Paul Hawken's book, *The Ecology of Commerce*. At the time, to say that Interface's business relied on petroleum would be dramatically understating the situation. Most synthetic fibers—like the nylon, polyester, and acrylic yarns that are woven into carpeting—are made out of petrochemicals. Ray's carpet tiles were also incredibly energy intensive to manufacture and distribute. Against this stark reality, and deeply moved by Hawken's vision of sustainable business, Ray made a profound decision: to completely eliminate oil from Interface's supply chain and all of its operations. When Ray brought this idea to his executive team, they thought it was a joke. Getting Interface off of oil was like getting a paper company off of trees, or a tire company off of rubber. It was more than a radical notion—it was borderline insanity.

In 1995, Ray made an unforgettable presentation at a major conference of Interface's largest investors. Dan Hendrix, Interface's then CFO and current CEO, recalled the incredible scene in a wonderful 2012 speech:

> There were about seventy-five people in the room, and about 80 percent of our shareholders were represented there. Ray had a slide tray with thirty-five slides in it—thirty-five slides that I had created to report on the company's financial picture. And on the morning of his presentation, Ray stood up, pushed the slide tray to the side, and said, "I'm not going to talk about my company today, I'm going to talk about Mother Earth. She's in trouble."
>
> Around the room, all I could see were looks of confusion that probably mirrored my own. Nobody knew what to do or say. Remember, these people [were] all about the bottom line—about financial results.
>
> Ray went on to tell the story of the reindeer of St. Matthew's Island, a story in Paul Hawken's *Ecology of Commerce* book that had so captivated him and opened his eyes. It's the story of a society—in this case, a society of reindeer—who within a twelve-year period of time overshot the carrying capacity of their island and entered a sharp period of decline that first decimated

their environment and then their population. It was a metaphor for Earth, and it struck him, he said, like a spear in the chest.

He set up the business case for sustainability as he imagined it—the end of oil, the scarcity of resources, the need to pioneer new technologies and new products that would win hearts and minds, and capture market share. Eliminate waste, get off oil.

The faces around the table went from confused to appalled. Needless to say, the reaction on the Street was swift and decisive. The next day, an analyst called to say that one of our largest shareholders was dumping the stock because, in his words, Ray had clearly lost his mind.

It wasn't just one investor who questioned Ray's sanity. In the days that followed Ray's presentation, the price of Interface's stock plummeted. But Ray stuck to his guns. He began to transform Interface's products and supply chain. Ray and his team devised new carpet materials that were lighter and less resource-intensive. Interface began a recycling program to keep old carpet tiles out of landfills, and it started using the old tiles it recovered to make new ones. The company invented a new production method called Cool Blue, which allowed Interface to recycle the old carpet tiles by heating nylon to a lower temperature to avoid degrading the material. Another Interface program called Net-Works reclaims and recycles nylon nets from fishing villages in the Philippines and Cameroon. Interface's engineers also embraced biomimicry. They noticed that on the forest floor, no square foot looks the same, but there is still harmony. With this principle in mind, they created new designs that allow single worn-out tiles to be replaced instead of needing to recarpet an entire room—reducing the amount of tiles needed and extending the life of their product.

Twenty years after Ray announced his company's transformation, Interface's progress is stunning. Today, 50 percent of Interface's raw materials are recycled or bio-based. The company's greenhouse gas emissions have declined by 73 percent since 1996, and its carbon footprint today is 22 percent lower than it was in 2008. Energy usage is down 40 percent. Water usage is down 87 percent. And Interface is well on its way to what it calls "Mission Zero"—the complete elimination of its corporate environmental impact by 2020.

The most remarkable thing about Interface's story, however, is that Ray didn't just transform his business from inherently wasteful to highly sustainable—he *doubled* it at the same time. By 2009, fifteen years after Ray's epiphany, the company had saved $450 million, and that money more than paid for all the investments Interface made in sustainable innovations. As Ray revealed in an incredible TED Talk (if you haven't seen it, you should!), sales had risen by 63 percent, and profits had doubled. What's more, Interface has been able to weather downturns better than its competitors, in part because it is not as impacted by rising energy and raw material costs.

Ray Anderson passed away in 2011. I was extraordinarily lucky to call him one of my mentors and my friend. In 1995, Ray spoke at one of USGBC's earliest meetings. He is as responsible as anyone for the success of the green building movement. There has truly never been a greater champion for sustainability in the private sector. That is a fact!

Ray rightly asked, "If business will lead, then who will lead business?" It's a pivotal question, particularly since a 2013 study found that two-thirds of all global warming emissions across history are traceable, ultimately, to just ninety corporations. It would be silly to argue that these companies and their leaders are especially *culpable,* given that we all use their products and contribute collectively to their environmental footprint. But it is so plainly obvious to see how these companies and their executives are especially *capable* of making a difference.

Who among our private sector leaders will choose the profitable future over the doomed present? Who will pick up the sustainability torch and lead industry forward? Who will be the next Ray Anderson?

By now, I hope you're convinced that profit can save the planet. But at the end of the day—or rather, by the end of this century—whether profit will or won't save the planet is entirely up to us. Unlike ecological evolution, in which nature selects survivors, in economic evolution, individuals have agency. Biological traits are passively inherited, but the strategies of businesses, activists, policy makers, and consumers are actively deliberated and chosen. Just like Ray Anderson, each of us can *decide* whether or not to evolve.

Ray was the very first leader of the sustainable industrial revolution. The future of the planet depends on how many people follow in his footsteps.

In the classic *Middlemarch*, George Eliot writes, "We are on a perilous margin when we begin to look passively at our future selves, and see our own figures led with dull consent into insipid misdoing and shabby achievement." We now stand on that perilous margin, looking out onto a future world in which we consent not just to "shabby achievement," but also to the "insipid misdoing" of institutional malpractice and environmental neglect. We cannot stand idly by and watch the coming great waves of climate change and economic peril wash over us like the floodwaters of now all-too-frequent storms and rising seas. We cannot allow our environment and our economy to be destroyed—on our watch—because of our passive resignation to a predictable downfall of our own making.

The choice is up to all of us, here on this "perilous margin," at every level of leadership, in every sector of society, in every corner of the world. We must choose revolution, for reasons both moral and monetary. Our balance sheets are hanging by a thread, while our civilization is hanging in the balance.

Profit can save the planet.

With your help, it will.

ACKNOWLEDGMENTS

Working in the sustainability movement for the past twenty-two years, I have been blessed to know and learn from many truly exceptional people, without whom I could have never written this book, and to whom I owe a debt of gratitude:

David Gottfried, who from day one has consistently supported my dream to become an authentic contributor to his ever-growing and important Green Building Big Idea . . .

Bill Browning, Kevin Stack, John Picard, Mark Ginsberg, Bob Fox, Gail Vittori, Scot Horst, Brendan Owens, and M.C. Antil, who taught me that Nature, Technology, Policy, Design, Human Health, Artistic Values, Supreme Thoughtfulness, and Creativity can in fact change the world . . .

The Volunteers, Board, Chapters, Committees, and Technical Champions of the U.S. Green Building Council, who have contributed in countless ways to this amazing movement . . .

My core team of Rachel, Roger (L&P), Kimberly, Peter, Taryn, Kate, Jim, Dave, Doug, Rhiannon, Chris, Jennifer, Nicolette, Alyssa, and the amazing Anna Grace . . .

Our entire USGBC/GBCI staff, who are my "DC Family," and who have given my life and my work the purpose I was always hoping for . . .

Judith Webb, who fearlessly and tirelessly has given my voice direction and discipline . . .

Ben Yarrow, Chris Fox, and West Wing Writers for never letting me give up on my *Greenthink* dream . . .

And Mahesh, my Indian Brother who has taught me so much about Business, Spirituality, and the global challenges related to the health and well-being of populations around the world.

Thank you all from the bottom of my heart.

—R.F.

BIBLIOGRAPHY

Author's Note

Borealis Centre for Environment and Trade Research. "Findings from the U.S. Book Industry: Environmental Trends and Climate Impacts." Commissioned by Book Industry Study Group and Green Press Initiative. 2008. Accessed September 2, 2015. http://www.greenpressinitiative.org /documents/trends_summary.pdf.

Foreword

Construction Intelligence Center. *Global Construction Outlook 2020*. February 2015.

McGraw Hill Construction. *World Green Building Trends*. Commissioned by United Technologies, U.S. Green Building Council, and World Green Building Council. 2013. Accessed September 28, 2015. http://www .worldgbc.org/files/8613/6295/6420/World_Green_Building_Trends _SmartMarket_Report_2013.pdf.

United Nations Environment Programme—Sustainable Buildings and Climate Initiative (UNEP SBCI). *Buildings and Climate Change: Summary for Decision-Makers*. Accessed September 2, 2015. http://www.unep.org /sbci/pdfs/SBCI-BCCSummary.pdf.

Introduction

Booz Allen Hamilton. *2015 Green Building Economic Impact Study*. Commissioned by U.S. Green Building Council. September 16, 2015.

Braterman, Paul S. "How Science Figured Out the Age of the Earth." *Scientific American*, October 20, 2013. Accessed September 2, 2015. http:// www.scientificamerican.com/article/how-science-figured-out-the-age -of-the-earth/.

Bush, George H. W. "Statement on Signing the Oil Pollution Act of 1990," August 18, 1990, *The American Presidency Project*, accessed September 2, 2015, http://www.presidency.ucsb.edu/ws/?pid=18772.

Hawken, Paul. *Blessed Unrest: How the Largest Social Movement in History Is Restoring Grace, Justice, and Beauty to the World*. New York: Penguin Books, 2008. 153.

Livermore, Michael, Elizabeth Piennar, and Jason A. Schwartz. *The Regulatory Red Herring: The Role of Job Impact Analyses in Environmental Policy Debates*. Institute for Policy Integrity. New York University School of Law. April, 2012. Accessed September 2, 2015. http://policyintegrity .org/files/publications/Regulatory_Red_Herring.pdf.

McKinsey & Company. "The Business of Sustainability: McKinsey Global Survey Results." October 2011. http://www.mckinsey.com/insights /energy_resources_materials/the_business_of_sustainability_mckinsey _global_survey_results.

National Aeronautics and Space Administration (NASA). "NASA, NOAA Find 2014 Warmest Year in Modern Record." January 16, 2015. Accessed September 2, 2015. http://www.nasa.gov/press/2015/january /nasa-determines-2014-warmest-year-in-modern-record.

National Oceanic and Atmospheric Administration—National Centers for Environmental Information (NOAA-NCDC). "Billion-Dollar U.S. Weather and Climate Disasters 1980–2014." Accessed September 2, 2015. http://www.ncdc.noaa.gov/billions/events.pdf.

"Billion-Dollar Weather and Climate Disasters: Overview." Accessed September 2, 2015. http://www.ncdc.noaa.gov/billions/.

"NCDC Releases 2012 Billion-Dollar Weather and Climate Disasters Information." Accessed September 2, 2015. https://www.ncdc.noaa .gov/news/ncdc-releases-2012-billion-dollar-weather-and-climate -disasters-information.

National Resources Defense Council. "Record-Breaking $17.3 Billion in Crop Losses Last Year; Significant Portion Potentially Avoidable." Press release. August 27, 2013. Accessed September 2, 2015. http://www.nrdc .org/media/2013/130827.asp.

Nick Wing. "Joe Manchin Shoots Cap-And-Trade Bill with Rifle in New Ad (VIDEO)." *Huffington Post*. October 11, 2010. Updated May 25, 2011. http://www.huffingtonpost.com/2010/10/11/joe-manchin-ad-dead -aim_n_758457.html.

Semple, Robert B., Jr. "Happy Birthday, Clean Water Act." *Taking Note* (editorial blog), *New York Times,* October 16, 2012, accessed September 2, 2015. http://takingnote.blogs.nytimes.com/2012/10/16/happy -birthday-clean-water-act/.

U.S. Environmental Protection Agency. "40th Anniversary of the Clean Air Act." Updated August 15, 2013. http://www.epa.gov/air/caa/40th.html.

"DDT Ban Takes Effect." Press release. December 31, 1972. Updated December 4, 2014. http://www2.epa.gov/aboutepa/ddt-ban-takes-effect.

U.S. Green Buildings Council. "About USGCB." Accessed September 2, 2015. http://www.usgbc.org/about.

Walsh, Mary Williams and Nelson D. Schwartz. "Estimate of Economic Losses Now Up to $50 Billion." *New York Times*, November 1, 2012. Accessed September 2, 2015. http://www.nytimes.com/2012/11/02 /business/estimate-of-economic-losses-now-up-to-50-billion.html ?adxnnl=1&adxnnlx=1435860344-LRaph1rcSNQsJZ844WH9Fw.

The World Bank and the Development Research Center of the State Council, the People's Republic of China. *China: 2030: Building a Modern, Harmonious, and Creative Society.* Washington, DC: World Bank, 2013. Accessed September 2, 2015. http://www.worldbank.org/content/dam /Worldbank/document/China-2030-complete.pdf.

World Health Organization. "7 Million Premature Deaths Annually Linked to Air Pollution." Press release. March 25, 2014. http://www.who.int /mediacentre/news/releases/2014/air-pollution/en/.

Chapter 2

Booz Allen Hamilton. *2015 Green Building Economic Impact Study.* Commissioned by U.S. Green Building Council. September 16, 2015.

Chapter 3

"2012 Wisconsin Presidential Results." *Politico.* Updated November 19, 2012. http://www.politico.com/2012-election/results/president/wisconsin/.

Bank of America. "Bank of America Tower at One Bryant Park is First Commercial Skyscraper in U.S. to Achieve LEED Platinum." Press release. May 20, 2010. http://newsroom.bankofamerica.com /press-release/environment/bank-america-tower-one-bryant-park-first -commercial-skyscraper-us-achieve-.

Berman, Scott. "Building Sustainable Schools." *School Planning and Management.* August 1, 2013. http://webspm.com/Articles/2013/08/01 /Building-Sustainable-Schools.aspx?admgarea=features&Page=2.

Booz Allen Hamilton. *2015 Green Building Economic Impact Study.* Commissioned by U.S. Green Building Council. September 16, 2015.

Chicago Park District. "Soldier Field Becomes First North American NFL Stadium to Attain LEED Certification." April 16, 2012. http://www .chicagoparkdistrict.com/soldier-field-becomes-first-north-american-nfl -stadium-to-attain-leed-certification/.

Content, Thomas. "Lake Mills Elementary Is Schooled in Green Building Design." *Milwaukee Wisconsin Journal Sentinel.* December 20, 2014. http://www.jsonline.com/business/lake-mills-elementary-is-schooled -in-green-building-design-b99411094z1-286466311.html.

Davis, Craig. "Marlins Park Wins 'Green' Award." *Sun Sentinel.* May 28, 2012. http://articles.sun-sentinel.com/2012-05-28/business/fl-green -miami-marlins-20120528_1_leed-gold-certification-rick-fedrizzi.

Dell Children's Medical Center of Central Texas. "Dell Children's First in the World to Earn LEED for Health Care Platinum Designation." July 10, 2013. http://www.dellchildrens.net/about_us/news/2013/07/10 /dell_childrens_first_in_the_world_to_earn_leed_for_health_care _platinum_designation.

"Energy & Atmosphere." Accessed September 2, 2015. https://www .dellchildrens.net/about_us/about_our_green_building/leeds_interactive _slideshow/#slide_12.

"Water Efficiency." Accessed September 2, 2015. https://www.dellchildrens .net/about_us/about_our_green_building/leeds_interactive_slideshow /#slide_11.

Eichholtz, Piet, Nils Kok, and Erkan Yonder. "Portfolio Greenness and the Financial Performance of REITs." *Journal of International Money and Finance.* 2012. http://www.fir-pri-awards.org/wp-content/uploads /Article-Eichhiltz-Kok-Yonder.pdf.

"The First Baseball Game." The Official Website for the State of New Jersey. Accessed September 2, 2015. http://www.state.nj.us/nj/about/baseball .html.

Florida Department of Environmental Protection. "Miami Marlins Knock Recycling Out of the Park." August 14, 2015. http://www.dep.state.fl.us /waste/quick_topics/publications/shw/recycling/recognition /MiamiMarlins2.pdf.

Gardner, Matt. "Lake Mills Elementary Nears Opening." *Lake Mills Leader.* August 14, 2014. http://www.hngnews.com/lake_mills_leader/news /school/article_c79cc036-23b9-11e4-84c0-0017a43b2370.html.

Harris, Debra D. "Return on Investments of a LEED Platinum Hospital: The Influence of Healthcare Facility Environments on Healthcare

Employees and Organizational Effectiveness." *Journal of Hospital Administration*, vol. 3, no. 6. (September 17, 2014). http://www.sciedu.ca /journal/index.php/jha/article/viewFile/5161/3296.

Kaiser Family Foundation. "Hospital Adjusted Expenses per Inpatient Day." Accessed September 2, 2015. http://kff.org/other/state-indicator /expenses-per-inpatient-day/.

Lake Mills School. "Lake Mills Area School District." Accessed September 2, 2015. http://www.lakemills.k12.wi.us/referendum/LM%20 Facility%20Committee%20Report%20to%20Board%20June%2011%20 2012.pdf.

"Lake Mills Middle School—First Public School in Nation to Achieve LEED Platinum." YouTube video. September 27, 2012. https://www .youtube.com/watch?v=_cjDYYNCACg.

McGraw Hill Construction. *World Green Building Trends.* Commissioned by United Technologies, U.S. Green Building Council and World Green Building Council. 2013. Accessed September 28, 2015. http://www .worldgbc.org/files/8613/6295/6420/World_Green_Building_Trends _SmartMarket_Report_2013.pdf.

Miami Marlins. "The Roof." Accessed September 2, 2015. http://miami .marlins.mlb.com/mia/ballpark/retractable_roof_facts.jsp.

"Year-by-Year Results." Accessed September 2, 2015. http://miami.marlins .mlb.com/mia/history/year_by_year_results.jsp.

"Middle School Ranks among Wisconsin's Greenest." *School Construction News.* June 14, 2011. http://www.schoolconstructionnews.com /articles/2011/06/14/middle-school-ranks-among-wisconsins-greenest.

Miron Construction. "Lake Mills Middle School." Accessed September 2, 2015. http://www.miron-construction.com/projects/121.

Sanke, Shirish et al. "India's Urban Awakening: Building Inclusive Cities, Sustaining Economic Growth," 207. McKinsey Global Institute. McKinsey & Company. April, 2010. http://www.mckinsey.com/insights /urbanization/urban_awakening_in_india.

Starbucks. *Global Responsibility Report 2014: What Is the Role and Responsibility of a For-Profit Public Company?* Report. http://globalassets.starbucks .com/assets/ea2441eb7cf647bb8ce8bb40f75e267e.pdf.

Ulrich, Roger S. "View Through a Window May Influence Recovery from Surgery." *Science*, vol. 224 (April 27, 1984): 420–21. https://mdc.mo.gov /sites/default/files/resources/2012/10/ulrich.pdf.

United Nations Environment Programme—Sustainable Buildings and Climate Initiative (UNEP SBCI). *Buildings and Climate Change: Summary for Decision-Makers*. Accessed September 2, 2015. http://www.unep.org/sbci/pdfs/SBCI-BCCSummary.pdf.

U.S. Green Building Council (USGBC). "One Bryant Park." Accessed September 2, 2015. http://www.usgbc.org/projects/one-bryant-park?view=overview.

Chapter 4

Morgan Stanley, Institute for Sustainable Investing. "The Business Case for Sustainable Investing." April 28, 2015. http://www.morganstanley.com/ideas/business-case-for-sustainable-investing/.

CALSTRS. "CalSTRS at a Glance." Accessed September 2, 2015. http://www.calstrs.com/glance.

Carlton, Jim. "California Drought Will Cost $2.2 Billion in Agriculture Losses This Year." *Wall Street Journal*. Updated July 15, 2014. http://www.wsj.com/articles/drought-will-cost-california-2-2-billion-in-losses-costs-this-year-1405452120.

Centers for Disease Control and Prevention. "Deaths Associated with Hurricane Sandy—October–November 2012." *Morbidity and Mortality Weekly Report*, vol. 62, no. 20 (May 24, 2013): 393–97. http://www.cdc.gov/mmwr/preview/mmwrhtml/mm6220a1.htm.

DeChant, Tim. "If the World's Population Lived Like . . ." *Per Square Mile*. August 8, 2012. http://persquaremile.com/2012/08/08/if-the-worlds-population-lived-like/.

Editorial staff. "Hurricane Sandy's Rising Cost." *New York Times*. November 27, 2012. http://www.nytimes.com/2012/11/28/opinion/hurricane-sandys-rising-costs.html.

Ernst and Young. "China and India: Tomorrow's Middle Classes." Accessed September 2, 2015. http://www.ey.com/GL/en/Issues/Driving-growth/Middle-class-growth-in-emerging-markets---China-and-India-tomorrow-s-middle-classes.

Food and Agriculture Organization of the United Nations—Statistics Division (FAO-STAT). "Food Balance Sheets." http://faostat3.fao.org/faostat-gateway/go/to/download/FB/FB/E.

Grossman, Gene M. and Alan B. Krueger. "Economic Growth and the Environment." *The Quarterly Journal of Economics*, vol. 110, no. 2 (May 1995): 353–77. http://www.econ.ku.dk/nguyen/teaching/Grossman%20and%20Krueger%201995.pdf.

"Environmental Impacts of a North American Free Trade Agreement." NBER Working Paper Series. National Bureau of Economic Research. Working Paper No. 3914. November 1991. http://www.nber.org/papers/w3914.pdf.

Gustin, Sam. "How Flooding in Thailand Hurts Intel's Sales." *Time*. December 13, 2011. http://business.time.com/2011/12/13/how -flooding-in-thailand-hurts-intels-sales/.

Hardin, Garrett. "The Tragedy of the Commons." *Science*, vol. 162, no. 3859 (December 13, 1968): 1243–48. http://cecs.wright.edu/~swang/cs409 /Hardin.pdf.

Houshi. "Home." Accessed September 2, 2015. http://www.ho-shi.co.jp /jiten/Houshi_E/home.htm.

"Master." Accessed September 2, 2015. http://www.ho-shi.co.jp/jiten /Houshi_E/master.htm.

Hower, Mike. "Report: Environmental Externalities Cost Global Economy $4.7 Trillion Annually." *Sustainable Brands*, April 22, 2013. http:// www.sustainablebrands.com/news_and_views/articles/report-top-100 -environmental-externalities-cost-global-economy-47-trillion-a.

Insurance Information Institute. "Hurricanes." Accessed September 2, 2015. http://www.iii.org/fact-statistic/hurricanes.

"Japanese Economy Shrank in Fourth Quarter." *Guardian*. February 13, 2012. http://www.theguardian.com/business/2012/feb/13/japan-economy -shrank-fourth-quarter.

Jervis, Rick. "Bastrop, Texas, Still Sees Hope Seven Months After Fire." *USA Today*. Updated April 25, 2012, http://usatoday30.usatoday.com /weather/wildfires/story/2012-04-24/bastrop-texas-wildfire/54515990/1.

Kuznets, Simon. "Economic Growth and Income Inequality." *The American Economic Review* vol. 45, no. 1 (March 1955). https://www.aeaweb.org /aer/top20/45.1.1-28.pdf.

"Simon Kuznets—Biographical." *Nobel Lectures, Economics 1969–1980*. Edited by Assar Lindbeck. Singapore: World Scientific Publishing Co. 1992. Accessed September 2, 2015. http://www.nobelprize.org/nobel _prizes/economic-sciences/laureates/1971/kuznets-bio.html.

Lubber, Mindy. "Climate-Proofing the Insurance Industry." *Forbes*. October 11, 2012. http://www.forbes.com/sites/mindylubber/2012/10/11 /climate-proofing-the-insurance-industry/.

Mills, Evan. "The Greening of Insurance." *Science*, vol. 338, no. 14 (December 14, 2012). http://evanmills.lbl.gov/pubs/pdf/science-2012-mills -1424-5.pdf.

Morgan Stanley—Institute for Sustainable Investing. "Sustainable Investing's Performance Potential." April 2, 2015. http://www.morganstanley.com /ideas/sustainable-investing-performance-potential/.

"Sustainable Reality: Understanding the Performance of Sustainable Investment Strategies." Report. March 2015. https://www.morganstanley .com/sustainableinvesting/pdf/sustainable-reality.pdf.

National Resources Defense Council. "Record-Breaking $17.3 Billion in Crop Losses Last Year; Significant Portion Potentially Avoidable." August 27, 2013. http://www.nrdc.org/media/2013/130827.asp.

O'Hara, William T. *Centuries of Success: Lessons from the World's Most Enduring Family Business.* Avon, MA: Adams Media, 2004. 17–21.

Pezzini, Mario. "An Emerging Middle Class." *OECD Observer*, 2012. http:// www.oecdobserver.org/news/fullstory.php/aid/3681/.

Schiller, Ben. "$4.7 Trillion: The Environmental Cost of Business." *FastCoExist.* April 23, 2013. http://www.fastcoexist.com/1681883/47 -trillion-the-environmental-cost-of-business.

Shabecoff, Philip. *A Fierce Green Fire: The American Environmental Movement.* Revised Edition. Washington, DC: Island Press, 2003. 27–28.

Smith, Adam. *An Inquiry into the Nature and Causes of the Wealth of Nations.* Kindle edition. Chicago: University of Chicago Press, 2012. Location 438–40.

Stabrawa, Anna, ed. "Recent Trends in Material Flows and Resource Productivity in Asia and the Pacific." United Nations Environment Programme. June 2013. http://www.unep.org/pdf/RecentTrendsAP(FinalFeb2013) .pdf, 8.

Tercek, Mark R. and Jonathan S. Adams. *Nature's Fortune: How Business and Society Thrive by Investing in Nature.* New York: Basic Books, 2013. 170.

UNEP Finance Initiative. "Pricing Environmental Damage: US$28 Trillion by 2050." Principles for Responsible Investment, October 6, 2010. http://www.unpri.org/press/pricing-environmental-damage-28 -trillion-by-2050-2/.

U.S. Environmental Protection Agency. "Inventory of U.S. Greenhouse Gas Emissions and Sinks: 1990–2012." April 15, 2015. 2–18. http://www3 .epa.gov/climatechange/Downloads/ghgemissions/US-GHG-Inventory -2015-Main-Text.pdf.

Walsh, Bryan. "The Costs of Climate Change and Extreme Weather Are Passing the High-Water Mark." *Time.* July 17, 2013. http://science.time

.com/2013/07/17/the-costs-of-climate-change-and-extreme-weather
-are-passing-the-high-water-mark/#ixzz2cjjHoL4w.

Walsh, Mary Williams and Nelson D. Schwartz. "Estimate of Economic
Losses Now Up to $50 Billion." *New York Times*. November 1, 2012.
http://www.nytimes.com/2012/11/02/business/estimate-of-economic
-losses-now-up-to-50-billion.html?adxnnl=1&adxnnlx=1435860344
-LRaph1rcSNQsJZ844WH9Fw.

Yandle, Bruce, Maya Vijayaraghavan, and Madhusudan Bhattarai. *The Environmental Kuznets Curve: A Primer*. PERC Research Study 02-1. May
2002. http://www.macalester.edu/~wests/econ231/yandleetal.pdf.

Yonder, Jamie, Anand Rao, and Mansoor Bajowala. "Insurance 2020: Turning
Change into Opportunity." PricewaterhouseCoopers. January 2012.
http://www.pwc.com/en_GX/gx/insurance/pdf/insurance-2020-turning
-change-into-opportunity.pdf.

Zabarenko, Deborah. "Water Use Rising Faster Than World Population."
Reuters. October 25, 2011. http://www.reuters.com/article/2011/10/25
/us-population-water-idUSTRE79O3WO20111025.

Chapter 5

The Association of Food, Beverage, and Consumer Products Company
(GMA) and Deloitte. "Finding the Green in Today's Shoppers: Sustainability Trends and New Shopper Insights." *GMA Online* (2009), 5, 6.
Accessed September 28, 2015. http://www.gmaonline.org/downloads
/research-and-reports/greenshopper09.pdf.

Bachman, Kate. "Dell's Campbell: The Whole Package." Sustainable Manufacturer Network. September 27, 2012. http://sustainablemfr.com
/materials/dells-campbell-whole-package.

Balch, Oliver. "Natura Commits to Sourcing Sustainability from Amazon."
Guardian. March 18, 2013. http://www.theguardian.com/sustainable
-business/natura-sourcing-sustainably-from-amazon.

Boechat, Cláudio and Roberta Mokrejs Paro. "Natura's Ekos: Perfume
Essences Produce Sustainable Development in Brazil." United Nations
Development Program, Growing Inclusive Markets. September 2007.
http://growinginclusivemarkets.org/media/cases/Brazil_Natura_2008.pdf.

Blériot, Joss. "Ford Motor Company River Rouge Production Plant (Michigan, USA)." Ellen MacArthur Foundation. August 20, 2010. http://
www.ellenmacarthurfoundation.org/business/articles/case-study-ford
-motor-company-river-rouge-production-plant-michigan-usa.

Bonini, Sheila and Hans-Werner Kaas. "Building a Sustainable Ford Motor Company: An Interview with Bill Ford."*McKinsey Quarterly* (January 2010). http://www.mckinsey.com/insights/sustainability/building_a _sustainable_ford_motor_company_an_interview_with_bill_ford.

Campbell, Oliver. Interview by Anne Marie Mohan. "Packaging World." *Packworld.* September 7, 2012. http://www.packworld.com /sustainability/renewable-resources/dell-powering-possible-green.

Con Edison. "Electricity." Accessed September 2, 2015. http://www.coned .com/history/electricity.asp.

Dailey, Jessica. "Empire State Building Achieves LEED Gold Certification." *Inhabitat New York City.* September 14, 2011. http://inhabitat.com/nyc /empire-state-building-achieves-leed-gold-certification/.

Dell. *An Annual Update on Our 2020 Legacy of Good Plan: FY15 Corporate Social Responsibility Report,* 39, 50. Accessed September 17, 2015. http://i.dell.com/sites/doccontent/corporate/corp-comm/en /Documents/fy15-cr-report.pdf.

"Bamboo—Nature's Eco-Friendly Packaging Solution." http://www.dell .com/learn/us/en/uscorp1/corp-comm/bamboo-packaging?c=us&l=en&s =corp&delphi:gr=true.

Empire State Realty Trust. "Historical Timeline." Empire State Building website. Accessed September 2, 2015. http://www.esbnyc.com/explore /historical-timeline.

"Innovative Empire State Building Program Cuts $7.5M in Energy Costs Over Past Three Years." Press release. August 14, 2014. http://www .esbnyc.com/sites/default/files/esb_year_three_press_release_final.pdf.

Frodl, Deb. "Ecomagination Progress." *GE Sustainability.* Accessed September 2, 2015. http://www.gesustainability.com/2014-performance /ecomagination/.

Gonzalo, Brujó, et al. "Best Retail Brands 2014," Interbrand, 117, 121. http://www.interbrand.com/assets/uploads/Interbrand-Best-Retail -Brands-2014-3.pdf (also listed at http://www.prnewswire.com /news-releases/interbrand-releases-the-2014-best-retail-brands -report-254348521.html).

Johnson Controls. "Honoring Our Past." Slideshow (slides 1, 3, 5, 8). Accessed September 2, 2015. http://www.jcihost.com/125th/index .html?lang=ENG#/timeline.

Kiron, David, et al. *The Innovation Bottom Line* (MIT Sloan Management Review and The Boston Consulting Group: Winter 2013), 8, accessed September 28, 2015, http://aca3318ae75562500643-ca1b2d270cca3d1f8

9a77092d5cd33a3.r63.cf2.rackcdn.com/MITSMR-BCG-Sustainability
-Report-2013.pdf.

Ling, Anthony, Sarah Forrest, Marc Fox, and Stephan Feilhauer. *Introduc-
ing GS Sustain*, Goldman Sachs, June 22, 2007, p. 4. https://www
.unglobalcompact.org/docs/summit2007/gs_esg_embargoed
_until030707pdf.pdf.

McGill, Alan. "Puma's Reporting Highlights Global Business Challenges."
PwC World Watch, Issue 3, 2011. Accessed September 28, 2015. http://
www.pwc.com/en_GX/gx/audit-services/corporate-reporting
/sustainability-reporting/assets/pumas-reporting-highlights-global
-business-challenges.pdf.

Mokyr, Joel. "The Second Industrial Revolution, 1870–1914." Northwestern
University: August 1998. http://faculty.wcas.northwestern.edu/~jmokyr
/castronovo.pdf.

"Natura Cosmeticos SA (NATU3:Sao Paulo)." *Bloomberg Business*. Accessed
September 2. 2012, https://outlook.office365.com/owa/#path=/mail
/sentitems.

Natura. "Sobre a Natura." Accessed September 2, 2015. Translated using
Google Translate/Chrome. http://www.natura.com.br/www/a-natura
/sobre-a-natura/.

PricewaterhouseCoopers. *Measuring and Managing Total Impact: A New
Language for Business Decisions (2013)*. Accessed September 17, 2015.
http://www.pwc.com/gx/en/sustainability/publications/total-impact
-measurement-management/assets/pwc-timm-report.pdf.

Procter and Gamble. "P&G Achieves Zero Manufacturing Waste at 45 Sites
Worldwide." Press release. April 2, 2013. http://news.pg.com/press
-release/pg-corporate-announcements/pg-achieves-zero-manufacturing
-waste-45-sites-worldwide.

Puma. *Business and Sustainability Report—Puma 2012*. Annual Report.
Accessed September 7, 2015. http://about.puma.com/damfiles/default
/sustainability/reports/puma-s-sustainability-reports/annual-reports
/PUMAGeschaeftsbericht2012_en-fa5c581a05cc3e5dd5502fa62a0ad4c2.pdf.

Puma Annual Report 2010. Accessed January 31, 2014. http://ir2.flife.de/data
/puma/igb_html/index.php?bericht_id=1000004&index=&lang=ENG.

"Puma Completes First Environmental Profit and Loss Account Which
Values Impacts at €145 Million." November 16, 2011. http://about
.puma.com/en/newsroom/corporate-news/2011/november/puma
-completes-first-environmental-profit-and-loss-account-which-values
-impacts-at-145-million-euro.

Siemens. "Facts and Figures." Accessed September 2, 2015. http://www
.siemens.com/about/sustainability/en/environmental-portfolio/Facts
-figures/.

Steer, Andrew. "Aligning Sustainability and Profit: What Are the Barriers?"
Guardian. March 20, 2013. http://www.theguardian.com/sustainable
-business/aligning-sustainability-profit-barriers-companies.

United Technologies Corporation. "Environment, Health, and Safety."
Accessed September 2, 2015. http://www.utc.com/Corporate
-Responsibility/Environment-Health-And-Safety/Pages/Default.aspx.

"Key Facts." Updated December 31, 2014. http://www.utc.com/Our
-Company/Pages/Key-Facts.aspx.

United Technologies Corporation—Aerospace Systems. "Space Systems."
Accessed September 2, 2015. http://utcaerospacesystems.com/cap
/systems/Pages/space-systems-business.aspx.

"United Technologies Corporation (NYSE: UTX)." Google Finance. https://
www.google.com/finance?chdnp=1&chdd=1&chds=1&chdv=1&chvs
=maximized&chdeh=0&chfdeh=0&chdet=1419973200000&chddm
=883660&chls=IntervalBasedLine&q=NYSE%3AUTX&ntsp
=0&fct=big&ei=19Z5VfC8JYaSmAGG04Fw.

Unilever. "Reducing Environmental Impact." Accessed September 2, 2015.
https://www.unilever.com/sustainable-living/the-sustainable-living-plan
/reducing-environmental-impact/.

"Sustainable Living." Accessed September 2, 2015. https://www.unilever
.com/sustainable-living/.

Making Sustainable Living Commonplace. Annual Report (2014). https://
www.unilever.com/Images/ir_Unilever_AR14_tcm244-421557.pdf.

"Unilever: In Search of the Good Business." *The Economist*. August 9, 2014.
http://www.economist.com/news/business/21611103-second-time-its
-120-year-history-unilever-trying-redefine-what-it-means-be.

Winston, Andrew. "Is the End of GE Capital Good News for Ecomagination?" *Harvard Business Review*. April 22, 2015. https://hbr.org/2015/04
/is-the-end-of-ge-capital-good-news-for-ecomagination.

Chapter 6

Anderlini, Jamil. "'Airpocalypse' Drives Expats Out of Beijing." *Financial
Times*. April 1, 2013. http://www.ft.com/intl/cms/s/0/46d11e30-99e9
-11e2-83ca-00144feabdc0.html?siteedition=intl#axzz2R8ajJzmV.

"Around 80 pc of Sewage in Indian Cities Flows into Water Systems." *Economic Times.* March 5, 2013. http://articles.economictimes. indiatimes.com/2013-03-05/news/37470083_1_untreated-sewage -water-sources-million-litres.

Beveridge & Diamond. "Latin American Region Environmental Report, Volume 1, 2013." 2012. http://www.bdlaw.com/assets/htmldocuments /April%202013%20LAR%20Report.pdf.

BioLite. "About Us—BioLite Stove." Accessed September 2, 2015. http:// dealerservices.biolitestove.com/about.html.

"BioLite HomeStove Program Now Live in Three Countries." July 13, 2013. http://www.biolitestove.com/blogs/lab/18676443-biolite-homestove -programs-now-live-in-three-countries.

"Mission." Accessed September 2, 2015. http://www.biolitestove.com/pages /mission.

"Overview." Accessed September 2, 2015. http://www.biolitestove.com /homestove/overview/.

Branigan, Tania. "China's Wen Jiabao Signs Off with Growth Warning." *Guardian*, March 5, 2013. http://www.theguardian.com/world/2013 /mar/05/china-wen-jiabao-growth-warning.

Carron, G. and A. Bordia, eds. *Issues in Planning and Implementing National Literacy Programs.* UNESCO: International Institute for Educational Planning (Paris: UNESCO, 1985), 47. http://unesdoc.unesco.org /images/0007/000765/076589eo.pdf.

"China Adopts New Plan, Highlights Emerging Industries as Drivers of Economic Growth." *The Clean Revolution.* June 14, 2012. http:// thecleanrevolution.org/news-and-events/news/china-adopts-new-plan -highlights-emerging-industries-as-drivers-of-economic-growth.

Collyns, Dan. "Peru Declares Environmental State of Emergency in Its Rainforest." *Guardian.* March 26, 2013. http://www.theguardian.com /environment/2013/mar/26/peru-declares-environmental-emergency -rainforest.

Davison, Nicola. "The Dead Pigs Rotting in China's Water Supply." *Guardian.* March 29, 2013. http://www.theguardian.com/world/2013/mar/29 /dead-pigs-china-water-supply.

Ferris, David. "Lessons in Sustainability from India's Entrepreneurs." *Forbes.* June 13, 2012. http://www.forbes.com/sites/davidferris/2012/06/13 /lessons-in-sustainability-from-indias-entrepreneurs/.

Ford, Edward. "Cost of Environmental Damage in China Growing Rapidly Amid Industrialization." *New York Times*. March 3, 2013. http://www .nytimes.com/2013/03/30/world/asia/cost-of-environmental -degradation-in-china is growing.html.

Ford, Peter. "Beijing Is Booming, but Talent Is Leaving Due to Bad Air." *Christian Science Monitor*. April 4, 2013. http://www.csmonitor.com /World/Asia-Pacific/2013/0404/Beijing-is-booming-but-talent-is -leaving-due-to-bad-air.

Fray, Keith. "China's Leap Forward: Overtaking the U.S. as World's Biggest Economy." *Financial Times* (blog). October 8, 2014. http://blogs.ft.com /ftdata/2014/10/08/chinas-leap-forward-overtaking-the-us-as-worlds -biggest-economy/.

Hannon, Allison, Ying Liu, Jim Walker, and Changhua Wu. "Delivering Low Carbon Growth: A Guide to China's 12th Five Year Plan." HSBC—The Climate Group. Executive Summary. March 2011. http:// www.theclimategroup.org/_assets/files/China-Five-Year-Plan -EXECUTIVE-SUMMARY.pdf.

Harrabin, Roger. "China 'Deserves More Credit,' for Renewable Energy Effort." *BBC News*. June 15, 2015. http://www.bbc.com/news /business-33143176.

Hoffman, Samantha and Jonathan Sullivan. "Environmental Protests Expose Weakness in China's Leadership." *Forbes*. June 22, 2015. http://www .forbes.com/sites/forbesasia/2015/06/22/environmental-protests -expose-weakness-in-chinas-leadership/.

Kaiman, Jonathan. "China Says More Than Half of Its Groundwater Is Polluted," *Guardian*, April 23, 2014, http://www.theguardian.com /environment/2014/apr/23/china-half-groundwater-polluted.

"China Unveils Details of Pilot-Carbon Trading Programme." *Guardian*. May 22, 2013. http://www.theguardian.com/environment/2013/may/22 /china-carbon-trading-shenzhen.

"Inside China's 'Cancer Villages.'" *Guardian*. June 4, 2013. http://www .theguardian.com/world/2013/jun/04/china-villages-cancer-deaths.

Lee, Carrie M., Chelsea Chandler, Michael Lazarus, and Francis X. Johnson. "Assessing the Climate Impacts of Cookstove Projects: Issues in Emissions Accounting." Stockholm Environment Institute. January 2013. http://sei-us.org/Publications_PDF/SEI-WP-2013-01-Cookstoves -Carbon-Markets.pdf.

Mani, Muthukumara. "India's Air Pollution Woes." World Bank (blog). March 25, 2013. http://blogs.worldbank.org/endpovertyinsouthasia/node/818.

Mukherjee, Krittivas. "Analysis: India Takes Unique Path to Lower Carbon Emissions." Reuters. http://www.reuters.com/article/2011/05/29/us-india-emissions-idUSTRE74S2PV20110529.

Plumer, Brad. "Coal Pollution in China Is Cutting Expectancy by 5.5 Years." *Washington Post.* July 8, 2013. http://www.washingtonpost.com/news/wonkblog/wp/2013/07/08/chinas-coal-pollution-is-much-deadlier-than-anyone-realized/.

Shou, Xin and Henry Sanderson. "Chinese Anger Over Pollution Becomes Main Cause of Social Unrest." *Bloomberg Business.* March 6, 2013. http://www.bloomberg.com/news/articles/2013-03-06/pollution-passes-land-grievances-as-main-spark-of-china-protests.

Stanway, David. "China Orders 7 Pilot Cities and Provinces to Set CO2 Caps." *Reuters.* January 13, 2012. http://www.reuters.com/article/2012/01/13/us-china-carbon-idUSTRE80C0GZ20120113.

T.P. "Beijing's Air Pollution." *Economist.* January 14, 2013. http://www.economist.com/blogs/analects/2013/01/beijings-air-pollution.

United Nations. "Chapter II—Poverty: The Official Numbers." *Inequality Matters: Report on the World Social Situation 2013.* New York: United Nations, 2013. 24.

The White House Office of the Press Secretary. "Fact Sheet: U.S.-China Joint Announcement on Climate Change and Clean Energy Cooperation." Press release. November 11, 2014. http://www.whitehouse.gov/the-press-office/2014/11/11/fact-sheet-us-china-joint-announcement-climate-change-and-clean-energy-c.

Wong, Chun Han. "More Than 82 Million Chinese Live on Less Than $1 a Day." *Wall Street Journal* (blog). October 15, 2014. http://blogs.wsj.com/chinarealtime/2014/10/15/more-than-82-million-chinese-live-on-less-than-1-a-day/.

Wong, Edward. "Air Pollution Linked to 1.2 Million Premature Deaths in China." *New York Times.* April 1, 2013. http://www.nytimes.com/2013/04/02/world/asia/air-pollution-linked-to-1-2-million-deaths-in-china.html?_r=0.

"In China, Breathing Becomes a Childhood Risk." *New York Times.* April 22, 2013. http://www.nytimes.com/2013/04/23/world/asia/pollution-is-radically-changing-childhood-in-chinas-cities.html.

World Bank. "China—Overview." Updated March 25, 2015. http://www
.worldbank.org/en/country/china/overview.

Ghana Country Environmental Analysis. Environment and Natural Resources
(AFTEN)—Africa Region, Report No. 36985-GH. November 2, 2007.
http://www-wds.worldbank.org/external/default/WDSContentServer
/WDSP/IB/2007/12/04/000020439_20071204092331/Rendered
/PDF/369850GH.pdf.

"India: Green Growth—Overcoming Environment Challenges to Promote
Development." March 6, 2014. http://www.worldbank.org/en/news
/feature/2014/03/06/green-growth-overcoming-india-environment
-challenges-promote-development.

*Nepal: Strengthening Institutions and Management Systems for Enhanced Envi-
ronmental Governance.* Report No: 38984–NP. World Bank: 2008.
http://www-wds.worldbank.org/external/default/WDSContentServer
/WDSP/IB/2008/04/09/000020439_20080409135430/Rendered
/PDF/389840white0cover0Nepal0CEA1webversion.pdf.

*Pakistan: Strategic Country Environmental Assessment (In Two Volumes) Volume
1: Main Report.* South Asia Environment and Social Development
Unit—South Asia Region, Report No. 36946-PK. August 21, 2006.
http://www-wds.worldbank.org/external/default/WDSContentServer
/WDSP/IB/2006/10/02/000160016_20061002113552/Rendered
/PDF/369461ovol011PK.pdf.

*Republic of Colombia: Mitigating Environmental Degradation to Foster Growth
and Reduce Inequality.* Environmentally and Socially Sustainable
Development Department—Latin America and the Caribbean Region,
Report No. 36345–CO. February 25, 2006. http://www.cepal.org/ilpes
/noticias/paginas/8/35988/colombia_cea_final.pdf.

"World Development Indicators." Accessed September 2, 2015. http://
databank.worldbank.org/data/reports.aspx?source=world-development
-indicators.

World Bank and the Development Research Center of the State Council,
the People's Republic of China. *China 2030: Building a Modern,
Harmonious, and Creative Society.* World Bank: March 23, 2013. http://
www-wds.worldbank.org/external/default/WDSContentServer
/WDSP/IB/2013/03/27/000350881_20130327163105/Rendered
/PDF/762990PUB0china0Box374372B00PUBLIC0.pdf.

World Health Organization. "Household Air Pollution and Health." March
2014. http://www.who.int/mediacentre/factsheets/fs292/en/.

Chapter 7

Bleich, Sara, Julia Wolfson, and Marian Jarlenski. "Indirect Effects From Menu Labeling Can Improve The Public's Health." *Health Affairs.* February 24, 2015. http://healthaffairs.org/blog/2015/02/24/indirect -effects-from-menu-labeling-can-improve-the-publics-health/.

Centers for Disease Control and Prevention. "CDC Study Finds Levels of Trans-Fatty Acids in Blood of U.S. White Adults Has Decreased." Press release. February 8, 2008. http://www.cdc.gov/media/releases/2012 /p0208_trans-fatty_acids.html.

Chandler, David. "Leaving Our Mark." *MIT News.* April 16, 2008. http:// news.mit.edu/2008/footprint-tt0416.

Chipotle Mexican Grill. "Chipotle Becomes the First National Restaurant Company to Use Only Non-GMO Ingredients." Press release. April 27, 2015. http://ir.chipotle.com/phoenix.zhtml?c=194775&p=irol -newsArticle&ID=2040322.

CNN Wire Staff. "Everyday Chemicals May Be Harming Kids, Panel Told." *CNN.* October 26, 2010. http://www.cnn.com/2010/HEALTH/10/26 /senate.toxic.america.hearing/.

Cohen, Adam. "100 Years Later, the Food Industry Is Still 'The Jungle.'" *New York Times.* January 2, 2007. http://www.nytimes.com/2007/01/02 /opinion/02tue4.html.

The Ecological Center. "Model Year 2011/2012 Guide to New Vehicles." February 2012. http://www.ecocenter.org/sites/default/files/2012_Cars .pdf.

Fenn, Donna, ed. "How I Did It: Stephen McDonnell of Applegate Farms." *Inc.* October 30, 2012. http://www.inc.com/magazine/201211/donna -fenn/stephen-mcdonnell-applegate-farms-a-household-name.html.

Ford, Dana and Lorenzo Ferrigno. "Vermont Governor Signs GMO Food Labeling into Law." *CNN.* May 8, 2008. http://www.cnn .com/2014/05/08/health/vermont-gmo-labeling/.

Global Real Estate Sustainability Benchmark. "About." Accessed September 2, 2015. https://www.gresb.com/about.

Grocery Manufacturers Association. "GMA Statement Regarding FDA's Notice on the (GRAS) Status of Partially Hydrogenated Oils (PHOs)." Press release. November 7, 2013. http://www.gmaonline.org/news -events/newsroom/gma-statement-regarding-fdas-notice-on-the-gras -status-of-partially-hydroge/.

Gutowski, Timothy, et al. "Environmental Life Style Analysis (ELSA)." MIT. Presented at *IEEE International Symposium on Electronics and the Environment*. May 19–20, 2008. http://web.mit.edu/ebm/www /Publications/ELSA%20IEEE%202008.pdf.

Harris, Melissa. "Chicago Gets New Method Soap Factory, Glimpse of Future with Fewer Workers." *Chicago Tribune*. April 28, 2015. http:// www.chicagotribune.com/business/ct-confidential-method-soap-0429 -biz-20150428-column.html

Hughlett, Mike. "Hormel Agrees to Buy Organic and Natural Meat Maker Applegate Farms." *Star Tribune*. May 27, 2015. http://www.startribune .com/hormel-agrees-to-buy-organic-and-natural-meat-maker-applegate -farms/305064971/.

Janssen, Wallace F. "The Story of the Laws Behind the Labels: Part 1—The 1906 Food and Drugs Act." *FDA Consumer*. June 1981. Via *Federal Department of Agriculture (FDA)*. Updated March 11, 2014. http://www .fda.gov/AboutFDA/WhatWeDo/History/Overviews/ucm056044.htm.

Kesmodel, David. "Hormel to Buy Organic Meat Maker for $775 Million." *Wall Street Journal*. May 26, 2015. http://www.wsj.com/articles/hormel -to-buy-organic-meat-maker-1432671859.

Kurtz, Rod. "A Soap Maker Sought Compatibility in a Merger Partner." *New York Times*. January 16, 2013. http://www.nytimes.com/2013/01/17 /business/smallbusiness/a-founder-of-the-soap-maker-method-discusses -its-sale.html?_r=0.

Ligteringen, Ernst. "Executive Perspective: Global Reporting Initiative's Chief Executive Ernst Ligteringen." *Sustainability* (blog). Thompson Reuters. April 11, 2013. http://sustainability.thomsonreuters .com/2013/04/11/executive-perspective-global-reporting-initiatives -chief-executive-ernst-ligteringen/.

McDonnell, Stephen. "Our Story." Applegate. Accessed September 2, 2015. http://www.applegate.com/our-story.

Method. "Beyond the Bottle." Accessed September 2, 2015. http:// methodhome.com/beyond-the-bottle/.

"Beyond the Bottle—Ingredients." Accessed September 2, 2015. http:// methodhome.com/beyond-the-bottle/ingredients/.

Morales, Lymari. "Green Behaviors Common in U.S., but Not Increasing." Gallup. April 9, 2010. http://www.gallup.com/poll/127292/green -behaviors-common-not-increasing.aspx.

National Cancer Institute. "Formaldehyde and Cancer Risk." June 10, 2011.
http://www.cancer.gov/about-cancer/causes-prevention/risk/substances
/formaldehyde/formaldehyde-fact-sheet.

Natural Resources Defense Council. "Take Out Toxics." Accessed September
2, 2015. http://www.nrdc.org/health/toxics.asp.

O'Connor, Anahad. "BPA in Cans and Plastic Bottles Linked to Quick
Rise in Blood Pressure." *Well* (blog), *New York Times*. December 8, 2014.
http://well.blogs.nytimes.com/2014/12/08/bpa-in-cans-and-plastic
-bottles-linked-to-quick-rise-in-blood-pressure/.

Plummer, Brad. "Poll: Scientists Overwhelmingly Think GMOs Are Safe
to Eat. The Public Doesn't." *Vox*. January 29, 2015. http://www.vox
.com/2015/1/29/7947695/gmos-safety-poll.

"President's Threat with Meat Report." *New York Times*. June 4, 1906.
Accessed September 2, 2015. http://query.nytimes.com/mem/archive
-free/pdf?res=9E05E2DC1231E733A25756C0A9609C946797D6CF.

Sinclair, Upton. "Worked on President's Sympathies—Sinclair."
Letter to the editor. *New York Times*. May 26, 1906.
http://query.nytimes.com/mem/archive-free/pdf?res
=9405E0DD1231E733A2575AC2A9639C946797D6CF.

Slater, Dashka. "How Dangerous Is Your Couch?" *New York Times*.
September 6, 2012. http://www.nytimes.com/2012/09/09/magazine
/arlene-blums-crusade-against-household-toxins.html.

Sustainable Accounting Standards Board. "Alignment." Accessed September
2, 2015. http://www.sasb.org/approach/key-relationships/.

Tracy, Tennille. "FDA Requires Calorie Counts at Restaurants." *Wall Street
Journal*. November 25, 2014. http://www.wsj.com/articles/federal
-government-to-mandate-more-calorie-counts-1416878402.

United Nations. *Report of the World Commission on Environment and
Development: Our Common Future* (n.d.). Accessed September 2, 2015.
http://www.un-documents.net/our-common-future.pdf.

Urbina, Ian. "Think Those Chemicals Have Been Tested?" *New York Times*.
April 13, 2013. http://www.nytimes.com/2013/04/14/sunday-review
/think-those-chemicals-have-been-tested.html.

U.S. Environmental Protection Agency. "Advancing Sustainable Materials Management: 2013 Fact Sheet Assessing Trends in Material Generation, Recycling and Disposal in the United States." Fact Sheet. June 2015. 3. http://
www.epa.gov/wastes/nonhaz/municipal/pubs/2013_advncng_smm_fs.pdf.

"Learn about Sustainability." Updated August 28, 2015. http://www2.epa .gov/sustainability/learn-about-sustainability#what.

"Toxic Substances Control Act." Updated June 27, 2012, http://www.epa .gov/agriculture/lsca.html.

"U.S. Greenhouse Gas Inventory Report: 1990–2013." April 2015. http:// www.epa.gov/climatechange/ghgemissions/usinventoryreport.html.

U.S. Food and Drug Administration (FDA). "History." Updated March 23, 2015. http://www.fda.gov/AboutFDA/WhatWeDo/History/.

"Milestones." December 19, 2014. http://www.fda.gov/AboutFDA /WhatWeDo/History/Milestones/ucm128305.htm.

U.S. Green Buildings Council. "Building Product Disclosure and Optimization—Environmental Product Declarations." Accessed September 2, 2015. http://www.usgbc.org/credits/new-construction-core-and-shell -schools-new-construction-retail-new-construction-healthca-22.

Whole Foods Market. "GMO: Your Right to Know." Accessed September 2, 2015. http://www.wholefoodsmarket.com/gmo-your-right-know.

Whorisky, Peter. "Is Your Food Genetically Modified? If Congress Moves on This, You May Never Know." *Washington Post.* March 25, 2015. http:// www.washingtonpost.com/news/wonkblog/wp/2015/03/25/is-your-food -genetically-modified-if-congress-moves-on-this-you-may-never-know/.

Chapter 8

Allen, Pam. "Ecovative Design Lands Deal with Crate & Barrel." Albany Business Review. November 14, 2011. http://www.bizjournals.com /albany/morning_call/2011/11/crate-barrel-using-ecovative.html.

Broder, John M. and Dan Frosch. "U.S. Delays Decision on Pipeline Until After Election." *New York Times.* November 10, 2011. http://www .nytimes.com/2011/11/11/us/politics/administration-to-delay-pipeline -decision-past-12-election.html?_r=0.

Bryce, Robert. "Is the Keystone XL Pipeline Worth Getting Arrested For?" *Slate.* February 20, 2013. http://www.slate.com/articles/health_and _science/science/2013/02/keystone_pipeline_protests_oil_companies _will_just_use_railroads.html.

Buford, Talia. "Pipeline Protestors Arrested at W.H." *Politico.* August 22, 2011. http://www.politico.com/news/stories/0811/61837.html.

Campbell, Oliver. "Dell's Cube, Content, Curb Approach to Packaging." Sustainable Brands. May 7, 2013. http://www.sustainablebrands.com/news _and_views/packaging/dells-cube-content-curb-approach-packaging.

Centers for Climate and Energy Solutions (C2ES). "Waxman-Markey Short Summary." Accessed September 2, 2015. http://www.c2es.org/federal /congress/111/acesa-short-summary.

Davenport, Coral. "Keystone Pipeline May Be Big, but This Is Bigger." *New York Times.* April 21, 2014. http://www.nytimes.com/2014/04/22 /business/energy-environment/us-emission-rules-would-far-outweigh -impact-of-keystone-pipeline.html.

"Report Opens Way to Approval for Keystone Pipeline." *New York Times.* January 31, 2014. http://www.nytimes.com/2014/02/01/us/politics /report-may-ease-way-to-approval-of-keystone-pipeline.html.

"U.S. Delays Final Call on Keystone XL Pipeline." *New York Times.* April 18, 2014. http://www.nytimes.com/2014/04/19/us/politics/us-delays -decision-on-keystone-xl-pipeline.html.

Davenport, Coral and Marjorie Connelly. "Most Republicans Say They Back Climate Action, Poll Finds." *New York Times.* January 30, 2015. http:// www.nytimes.com/2015/01/31/us/politics/most-americans-support -government-action-on-climate-change-poll-finds.html?emc=edit _na_20150130&nlid=60733578&_r=4.

Ecovative Design. "Automotive." Accessed September 2, 2015. http://www .ecovativedesign.com/products-and-applications/automotive/.

Elkins, James W. "Chlorofluorocarbons (CFCs)." National Oceanic and Atmospheric Administration, Climate Monitoring and Diagnostics Laboratory. Via *The Chapman & Hall Encyclopedia of Environmental Science.* Edited by David E. Alexander and Rhodes W. Fairbridge (Boston: Kluwer Academic, 1999). 78–80. http://www.esrl.noaa.gov /gmd/hats/publictn/elkins/cfcs.html.

Environmental Defense Fund. "McDonald's: Better Packaging." Accessed September 2, 2015. http://business.edf.org/projects/featured/past -projects/better-packaging-with-mcdonalds/.

"McDonald's and Environmental Defense Fund Mark 20 Years of Partnerships for Sustainability." November 15, 2010. https://www.edf .org/news/mcdonald%E2%80%99s-and-environmental-defense-fund -mark-20-years-partnerships-sustainability.

"McDonald's: The First Corporate Partnership." Accessed September 2, 2015. https://www.edf.org/partnerships/mcdonalds.

"Our Story: How EDF Got Started." Accessed September 2, 2015. https:// www.edf.org/about/our-history.

Fair, Matt. "TerraCycle Gets a Big Deal with Walmart." *Times of Trenton Regional News*. April 9, 2010. http://www.nj.com/news/times/regional /index.ssf?/base/news-19/1270791984132400.xml&coll=5.

Frazier, Ian. "Form and Fungus." *New Yorker*. May 20, 2013. http://www .newyorker.com/magazine/2013/05/20/form-and-fungus.

Gillis, Justin. "U.N. Says Lag in Confronting Climate Woes Will Be Costly." *New York Times*, January 16, 2014. http://www.nytimes.com/2014/01/17 /science/earth/un-says-lag-in-confronting-climate-woes-will-be-costly .html?hp&gwh=8B53D4B9D12FC9B6B4371BD1264CAED3&gwt=pay.

"U.S. Climate Had Already Changed, Study Finds, Citing Heat and Floods." *New York Times*. May 6, 2014. http://www.nytimes.com /2014/05/07/science/earth/climate-change-report.html?gwh =C6831AD8BBB13A11C4DD16F925DF30A2&gwt=pay&assetType =nyt_now.

Goldenberg, Suzanne. "Keystone XL Protestors Pressure Obama on Climate Change Promise." *Guardian*. February 17, 2013. http://www .theguardian.com/environment/2013/feb/17/keystone-xl-pipeline -protest-dc.

Goldstein, Eric. "New York Set to Ban Environmentally Troublesome Polystyrene Foam Coffee Cups and Food Containers—A Victory for Cleaner Streets, Parks and Waterways." *Switchboard* (blog), Natural Resources Defense Council, January 8, 2015, http://switchboard.nrdc .org/blogs/egoldstein/new_york_city_set_to_ban_envir.html.

Henly, Alice, Allen Hershkowitz, and Darby Hoover. *Game Changer: How the Sports Industry Is Saving the Environment*. Natural Resources Defense Council, 2012, p. 44, 50, http://www.nrdc.org/greenbusiness/guides /sports/files/Game-Changer-report.pdf.

Kline, Benjamin. *First Along the River: A Brief History of the U.S. Environmental Movement*. Lanham, MD: Rowman & Littlefield Publishers, 2011. 174.

Leber, Rebecca. "Republicans Are Furious About Obama's Climate Breakthrough With China." *New Republic*. November 12, 2014. http:// www.newrepublic.com/article/120246/us-china-2014-climate-deal -enrages-republican-politicians.

Lizza, Ryan. "As the World Burns." *The New Yorker*. October 11, 2010. http:// www.newyorker.com/magazine/2010/10/11/as-the-world-burns.

Miller, Hannah. "Patagonia Founder Takes Aim: 'The Elephant in the Room Is Growth.'" *GreenBiz*. March 1, 2013. http://www.greenbiz.com/news /2013/03/01/patagonia-founder-takes-aim-elephant-room-growth.

Molina, Mario J. and F. S. Rowland, "Stratospheric Sink for Chlorofluoro-methanes: Chlorina Atom-Catalysed Destruction of Ozone." *United Nations Environment Programme*. Via *Nature*, vol. 249, no. 5460. June 28, 1974. 810-12. http://www.unep.ch/ozone/pdf/stratopheric.pdf.

Nakamura, David and Steven Mufson. "China, U.S. Agree to Limit Green-house Gases." *Washington Post*. November 12, 2014. http://www.washingtonpost.com/business/economy/china-us-agree-to-limit-greenhouse-gases/2014/11/11/9c768504-69e6-11e4-9fb4-a622dae742a2_story.html.

Nock, Stephen. "Evocative Raises Over $14 Million of Equity Capital." Evocative Design. November 5, 2013, http://www.ecovativedesign.com/news/index.cfm?guid=8F0216CF2A036835311529B730C6AFE 01A9E7E895C891E4AE5CCF579F128BF4B762615A5371BA2B ECDBBA1ECAD9D0F65.

Pielke, Roger, Jr. "Climate of Failure." *Foreign Policy*. August 6, 2012. http://foreignpolicy.com/2012/08/06/climate-of-failure/.

Renshaw, Jarrett. "U.S. Taxpayers Help Fund Oil-Train Boom Amid Safety Concerns." Reuters. December 14, 2014. http://www.reuters.com/article/2014/12/14/us-railways-crude-insight-idUSKBN0JS0DR20141214.

Sealed Air Corporation, "Sealed Air and Ecovative Complete Agreement to Accelerate Commercialization of New Sustainable Packaging Material." Press release, Reuters, June 20, 2012, http://www.reuters.com/article/2012/06/20/idUS103149+20-Jun-2012+BW20120620.

Shogren, Elizabeth. "Protestors Call on Obama to Reject Keystone XL Pipe-line." *National Public Radio*. February 18, 2013. TransCanada. "Keystone XL Timeline." Accessed September 2, 2015. http://www.transcanada.com/social/responsibility/2011/keystone_xl/timeline/.

Stephenson, Emily. "Hundreds of Keystone Protestors Arrested at White House." *Reuters*, March 2, 2014. http://www.reuters.com/article/2014/03/03/us-usa-keystone-protest-idUSBREA210RI20140303.

Thau, Barbara. "Target Makes Big Push into Natural, Organic Market (Whole Foods' Sweet Spot) with 'Made to Matter." *Forbes*. April 9, 2014. http://www.forbes.com/sites/barbarathau/2014/04/09/target-makes-big-push-into-natural-organic-market-whole-foods-sweet-spot-with-made-to-matter/.

"TransCanada Intends Expansion of Keystone Pipeline." *Lincoln Journal Star*. July 16, 2008. http://journalstar.com/business/transcanada-intends-expansion-of-keystone-pipeline/article_b09a7ea5-3c1e-52c2-b159-29c29309a5fc.html.

Unilever. "FSI: Unilever's Fish Sustainability Initiative." Accessed September 2, 2015. https://www.unilever.com/Images/unilevers-fish-sustainability -initiative_tcm244-424822_1.pdf.

United Nations Environment Programme—Ozone Secretariat. "Treaties and Decisions." Accessed September 2, 2015. http://ozone.unep.org/en /treaties-and-decisions.

U.S. Environmental Protection Agency. "1990 Clean Air Act Amendment Summary." Updated September 15, 2015. http://www2.epa.gov/clean -air-act-overview/1990-clean-air-act-amendment-summary.

"Ozone Science: The Facts behind the Phaseout." Updated August 19, 2010. http://www.epa.gov/ozone/science/sc_fact.html.

"Health and Environmental Effects of Ozone Layer Depletion." Updated April 8, 2015. http://www3.epa.gov/ozone/science/effects/.

Walgate, R. "Futures: The Aerosol and Antarctica / Fears for the Ozone Layer." *Guardian.* May 30, 1985. https://www.nexis.com/results /enhdocview.do?docLinkInd=true&ersKey=23_T22315723343&format =GNBFI&startDocNo=0&resultsUrlKey=0_T22315723346&backKey =20_T22315723347&csi=138620&docNo=1).

Waxman, Henry (sponsor). "American Clean Energy and Security Act of 2009." Library of Congress. Introduced May 15, 2009. http://thomas.loc .gov/cgi-bin/bdquery/z?d111:HR02454:@@@X.

Wheaton, Sarah. "Nebraska: Judge Blocks Pipeline Route." *New York Times.* February 20, 2014. http://www.nytimes.com/2014/02/20/us/nebraska -judge-blocks-pipeline-route.html?_r=0.

The White House. "Federal Leadership on Climate Change and Environmental Sustainability—EXECUTIVE ORDER 13693." Accessed September 2, 2015. https://www.whitehouse.gov/administration/eop /ceq/sustainability.

The White House Office of the Press Secretary. "Fact Sheet: President Obama to Announce Historic Carbon Pollution Standards for Power Plants." Press release. August 3, 2015. https://www.whitehouse.gov/the -press-office/2015/08/03/fact-sheet-president-obama-announce-historic -carbon-pollution-standards.

"Fact Sheet: U.S.-China Joint Announcement on Climate Change and Clean Energy Cooperation." Press release. November 11, 2014. http://www .whitehouse.gov/the-press-office/2014/11/11/fact-sheet-us-china-joint -announcement-climate-change-and-clean-energy-c.

World Wildlife Fund. "History." Updated 2015. https://www.worldwildlife
.org/about/history.

"Harnessing Forces For Conservation—Overview." Updated 2015. http://
www.worldwildlife.org/initiatives/harnessing-forces-for-conservation.

"Overfishing—Overview." Updated 2015. http://www.worldwildlife.org
/threats/overfishing.

"Tuna—Overview." Updated 2015. http://www.worldwildlife.org/industries
/tuna.

Conclusion

Anderson, Ray. "The Business Logic of Sustainability." TED Talk (video).
15:54. February 2009. http://www.ted.com/talks/ray_anderson_on_the
_business_logic_of_sustainability.

"The Journey from There to Here—The Eco-Odyssey of a CEO." Keynote
Address. U.S. Green Building Conference. Big Sky, Montana. August 14,
1995. http://www.interfaceglobal.com/pdfs/ECO_ODYSSEYbooklet
_Sept2011.aspx.

Eliot, George. *Middlemarch*. Kindle edition. July 1994. Location 962.

Goldenberg, Suzanne. "Just 90 Companies Caused Two-Thirds of Man-Made
Global Warming Emission." *Guardian*. November 20, 2013. http://www
.theguardian.com/environment/2013/nov/20/90-companies-man-made
-global-warming-emissions-climate-change.

Hendrix, Dan T. "Keynote." Address, U.S. Chamber of Commerce. Atlanta.
April 2012.

Interface Global. "All Metrics." Accessed September 2, 2015. http://www
.interfaceglobal.com/Sustainability/Our-Progress/AllMetrics.aspx.

"Biomimicry—Learning from Nature." Accessed September 2, 2015. http://
www.interface.com/US/en-US/about?cmsContent=%2Fcarpet%
2FBiomimicry.html.

"Interface's History." http://www.interfaceglobal.com/company/history.aspx.

"Mission Zero." Accessed September 2, 2015, http://www.interfaceglobal
.com/careers/mission_zero.html.

"Net-works." Accessed September 2, 2015. http://net-works.com/.

Vitello, Paul. "Ray Anderson, Businessman Turned Environmentalist, Dies at 77."
New York Times. August 10, 2011. http://www.nytimes.com/2011/08/11
/business/ray-anderson-a-carpet-innovator-dies-at-77.html?_r=0.

Posner, Bruce G. "One CEO's Trip from Dismissive to Convinced." *MIT Sloan Management Review*. October 1, 2009. http://sloanreview.mit.edu /article/one-ceos-trip-from-dismissive-to-convinced/.

The Ray C. Anderson Foundation. "Biography." Accessed September 2, 2015. http://www.raycandersonfoundation.org/biography.

INDEX

U.S. Food and Drug Administration
(FDA), 120
U.S. Green Building Council
(USGBC)
about, xii, 1–3
accused of selling out, 28
Greenbuild conference and expo,
158
green building movement and,
11–12
mission, 24
startup, 24–29
transparency, promotion of, 128
See also specific topics and persons
utility bills and Marlins Park, 51

value and transformation, 61–63
volatile organic compounds (VOCs),
126

Watson, Rob, 30
Waxman-Markey bill, 147
Wealth of Nations (Smith), 60–61

weather and climate disasters, 6–7,
66–69. *See also* climate change
WELL Building Standard, 33–34
Wen Jiabao, 99
Whole Foods Market, 85, 119
Wiley, Harvey Washington, 120
Wiley Act (Pure Food and Drug
Act), 122
women's rights movement, 135–136,
138
World Bank
on China, 7, 92, 98
Country Environmental Analyses
(CEAs), 102–103
EDGE program, 32
on India, 102
World Health Organization
(WHO), 7, 107
World Wildlife Fund (WWF), 152

Xi Jinping, 100

ABOUT THE AUTHOR

 Since cofounding the U.S. Green Building Council in 1993 and serving as its CEO since 2004, Rick Fedrizzi has helped create the global movement for sustainable buildings and communities. He oversaw the creation of LEED (Leadership in Energy and Environmental Design), the world's premier green building program, which certifies almost two million square feet of sustainable building space per day in more than 150 countries and has accredited nearly 200,000 LEED professionals worldwide.

Rick is also CEO of Green Business Certification Inc. and the chair of the Global Real Estate Sustainability Benchmark. Additionally, he serves on numerous boards and advisory committees for diverse organizations, including Harvard University's T. H. Chan School of Public Health; the Clinton Global Initiative; Bank of America; Global Green; and DELOS.

Rick was previously an executive with Carrier, a United Technologies Corporation subsidiary, for twenty-five years.

A native of Syracuse, New York, he holds a BA from Le Moyne College and an MBA from Syracuse University. Rick and his wife, Cathy, a public school teacher and lifelong educator, live in Syracuse.